▼ Quick & Easy ▼
CUSTOM CABINETS

▼ Quick & Easy ▼

CUSTOM CABINETS

ANTHONY GUIDICE

STERLING PUBLISHING CO., INC. • New York

Library of Congress Cataloging-in-Publication Data

Guidice, Anthony

Quick and easy custom cabinets/Anthony Guidice.

p. cm.

Includes index.

ISBN 0-8069-8725-1

1. Cabinetwork—Amateurs' manuals. 2. Woodwork—equipment and supplies.

TT197 .G82 2002

684. 1'6—dc21   2001049749

Published by Sterling Publishing Company, Inc.

387 Park Avenue South, New York, N.Y. 10016

© 2002 by Anthony Guidice

Distributed in Canada by Sterling Publishing

c/o Canadian Manda Group, One Atlantic Avenue, Suite 105

Toronto, Ontario, Canada M6K 3E7

Distributed in Great Britain and Europe by Cassell PLC

Wellington House, 125 Strand, London WC2R 0BB, England

Distributed in Australia by Capricorn Link (Australia) Pty Ltd.

P.O. Box 704, Windsor, NSW 2756 Australia

Sterling ISBN 0-8069-8725-1

Drawings by Anthony Guidice
Photography by Vicki Guidice
Designed by Chris Swirnoff
Edited by Michael Cea

DEDICATION

One day, in late 1974, on the north side of Columbia, Missouri,
a college English teacher turned me into a writer.

This book is for Penelope (Carroll) Braun

*" If you treat an individual...as if he were what he ought to be and could be,
he will become what he ought to be and could be."*

JOHANN WOLFGANG VON GOETHE

Contents

▼

Chapter 3: Biscuit-Jointing and Assembling Carcasses and Face Frames 45

PART TWO
Building a
Cabinet
Step by Step

Chapter 4: Building the Carcass 61

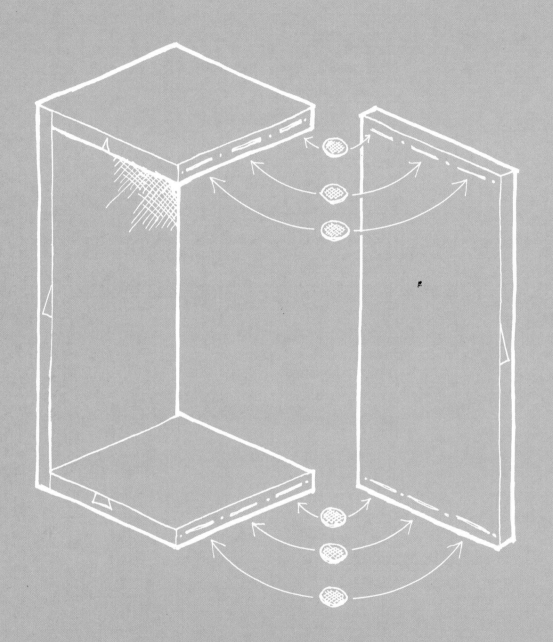

Introduction

▶ This book describes a simple, fast, and accurate method of making cabinets. It is not a comprehensive study of how to make a complete kitchen full of cabinets of all sorts; nor is it a book on any one specific type of cabinet—a gun case say, or a display case for carvings or trophies. This book is about a very efficient technique, covered very thoroughly.

For clarity, the information that follows is divided into two parts. Part One discusses the traditional methods of building cabinets, and their drawbacks: lengthy setup time, difficult assembly, questionable strength. Then it moves to a discussion of my technique, and its advantages: very fast setup time, great strength, and ease of assembly. This technique can be used on both *carcass* and *frame* construction.

Part One also examines the tools needed to build cabinets. Most of this equipment you probably already own. The primary tool required is the biscuit jointer*. Since there can be confusion about which biscuit jointer is best, and what features are important, a few different models are described. However, just about any biscuit jointer currently available can be used. Some shop-made accessories that help in cabinetmaking are also covered, with instructions on how to make them.

They are also known as biscuit joiners.

Part One also shows how to make carcass and frame joints using this technique. This covers layout and the specifics of assembly particular to each joint.

Part Two details the step-by-step construction of a specific cabinet. This cabinet is 15 x 31½ inches, with a face frame, frame-and-panel door, adjustable shelf, and one drawer. It is a general-purpose cabinet, usable for any number of things: workshop storage, laundry room, etc. The design is such that not only will you be able to build a practical cabinet but you will learn my method of building one easily and expeditiously. Later, you may wish to build cabinets with more drawers or with no drawers, display cabinets, entertainment centers, or bathroom medicine chests, etc. You will have the foundation to do this.

Part Two first examines *carcass construction*, that is, how to make the "box" (**I–1**). This is the basic building block for many woodworking projects. Then frame construction is covered, including the construction of the face frame and the frame-and-panel door (**I–2**). The next chapter shows how to make and fit a drawer to the cabinet using the same biscuit-jointer method.

It's important to make the cabinet to familiarize yourself with the technique. Once the cabinet is completed, you will have learned enough about the method to enable yourself to make

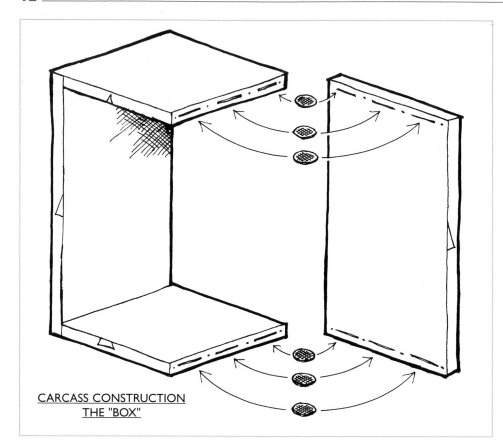

CARCASS CONSTRUCTION
THE "BOX"

I–1. The quick and easy method used to join a side (vertical) with top and bottom members (horizontal).

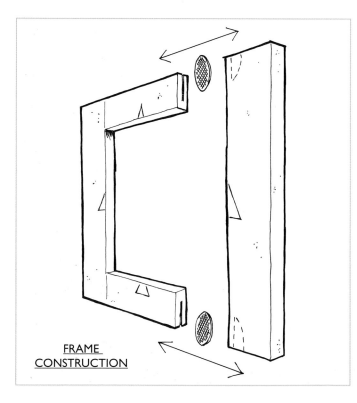

FRAME
CONSTRUCTION

any type of cabinet you like. The ideas here are fully flexible and adaptable to any type of cabinet construction (**I–3** to **I–8**).

The reason I don't give exact dimensions for this cabinet construction is because every craftsman's methods are a little different, and cabinets made by different people will vary slightly—even though the measurements are the same. Saws differ, wood differs, working methods differ.

As you read through the book, you'll notice that there are repetitions. These are intentional and are related to the thorough understanding of the cabinetmaking concept. For

I–2. The quick and easy method used to join face-frame or door stiles (vertical) to rails (horizontal).

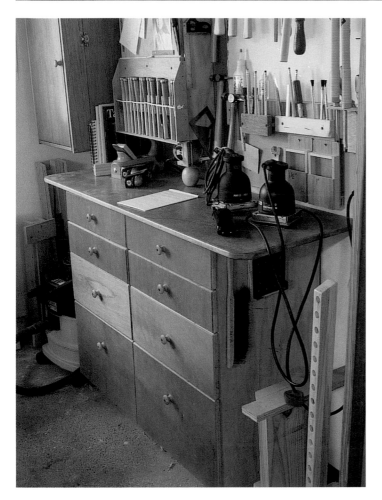

1–3 (above left). This workshop cabinet sits next to my bench. Eight drawers hold measuring items, power tools, glue, biscuits, nails, etc.

1–4 (above right). Two workshop storage cabinets. The narrow one with drawers was custom-made for the small area it occupies.

1–5. An installed bathroom wall unit made to hold towels and linens. The materials used were white pine and lauan plywood.

this reason, it is essential that the book be read and followed in sequential order. If you skip about from place to place, you may be confused.

While reading the book, there may seem to be questions that appear to be left unanswered. I find it best to not stray from the main point at hand, and to pick up the loose ends later on. Hence an additional reason for reading the book in order.

Anthony Guidice

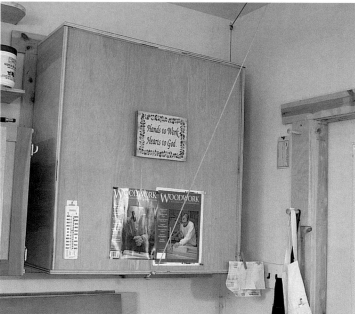

I–6 and I–7(above). The method of cabinetmaking described in the following pages can be used to build a wide assortment of cabinets, including this one, which is actually a cover for a louvered wall fan.

I–8 (right). A combination drawer unit and bookshelf. Note the plugs on the side of the cabinet.

▼ Quick & Easy ▼

CUSTOM CABINETS

PART ONE

Cabinet-Making Fundamentals

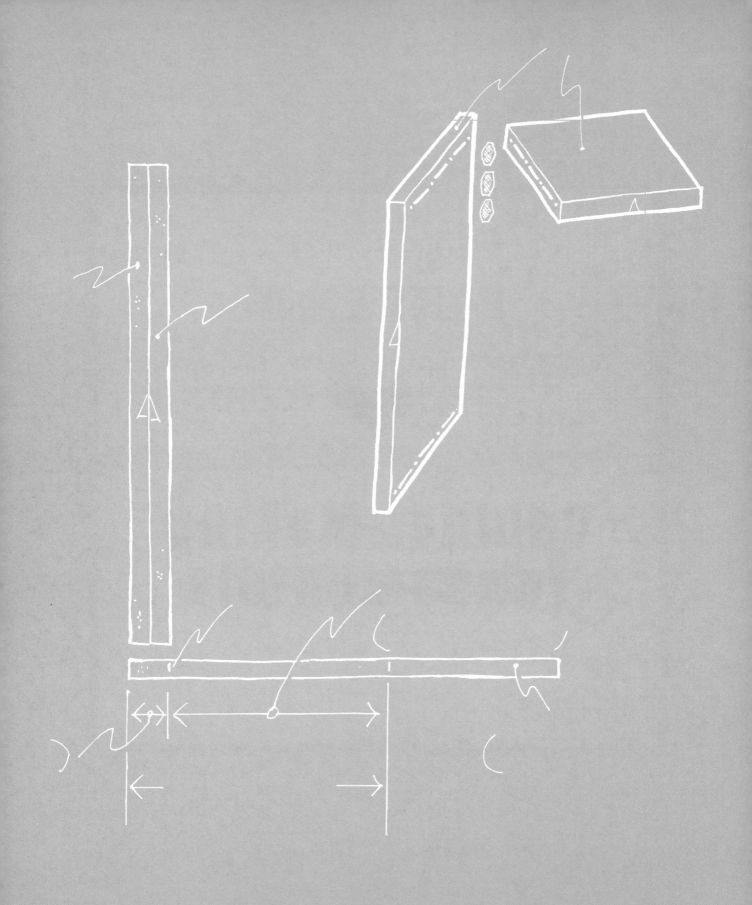

Cabinet Construction: A Primer

▶ Modern technology in power tools—specifically the coming of age of the biscuit jointer—has rendered most traditional cabinetmaking methods obsolete. With a biscuit jointer and a power drill, you can make cabinets in at least half the time it previously took. Not only that, but the finished product can be made more accurately and much stronger than before.

This method also makes the planning and logistics of large cabinetmaking projects such as a kitchen infinitely easier. Rather than having to buy all the material, make all the dimensional and joinery cuts at once, and then assemble everything at the end (and heaven help you if you miscalculated the slightest detail beforehand!), this method allows you to easily build one cabinet at a time. That means you'll need less space and material.

I developed this approach to cabinetmaking when I was living in St Louis. I needed to build cabinets for a kitchen in a very tiny shop. Standard production methods were out of the question. I had to rough-cut the plywood to just get it *into* the shop, much less buy and store ten sheets at a time. Because of these space restrictions, I obviously couldn't cut all the parts for all

the cabinets at once either. These limitations turned out to be a great blessing, because the method I eventually devised—which is the one covered in this book—worked out so well I've used it for all subsequent kitchen cabinet jobs, and almost all other cabinet work as well.

In order to understand the efficiency of this technique I'll be covering, let's take a look at the traditional method.

▼ TRADITIONAL CABINET CONSTRUCTION

Traditional cabinetmaking techniques require the woodworker to become a one-person mini-factory, an assembly-line worker. The traditional method used to join cabinets together is by tongue and groove. A groove is milled in the sides of the cabinet (the vertical members), and a tongue is cut on the ends of the horizontal members. A "shouldered joint" is preferred to a nonshouldered one (1–1) because of the mechanical strength it affords, but this still remains a flawed way to work, for several reasons.

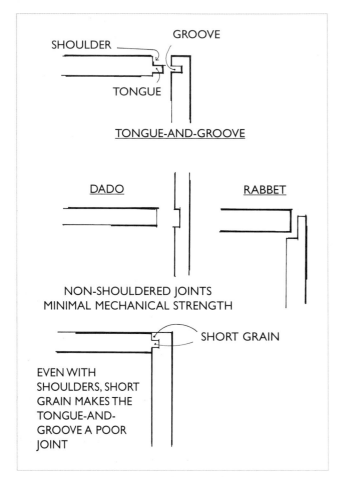

1–1. *"Shouldered" and "non-shouldered" joints.*

1–2. *A tongue-and-groove carcass can easily rack out of square.*

The main disadvantage of tongue-and-groove joinery for cabinets is that it's a weak joint. The short grain both on the tongue and the groove doesn't allow much mechanical support. You can easily rack the cabinet (**1–2**), and even crack the tongue by pushing down on one corner. Nailing a ¼-inch plywood back to the cabinet and attaching the face frame make for a stronger cabinet if you use this joinery. The tongue-and-groove joint used for frame construction is stronger (**1–3**), but not much.

The tongue-and-groove joint is also difficult and time-consuming to make and to fit. A shaper is the best way to make a tongue, but how many of us have a shaper? Even if we do, a shaper is time-consuming to set up and the tooling is expensive.

A dado head on a table saw is best for the groove. A stack dado head for a table saw takes a lot of time to set for the right width cut and to mount on the saw. A wobble dado head can be quickly adjusted, but once it's set, you can't take it off the saw without losing the setting. You could use a handheld router and an edge guide to cut the grooves, and perhaps set the table saw up to cut the tongues, but if the plywood varies in dimension from sheet to sheet and/or you don't feed it perfectly, the tongues won't fit the grooves anymore. Seems like a lot of setup time and work for a weak joint.

Once you have *all* these machines set up to cut tongues or grooves, there is an additional disadvantage: You need to cut the tongues or grooves on all the pieces. There is too much setup time involved to do otherwise. So, if you're making more than one cabinet, your shop is tied up with one job until all the pieces are cut. Heaven help you if you measured something wrong or if one of your settings is off a little, or some other miscalculation. You will have a pile of cabinet parts

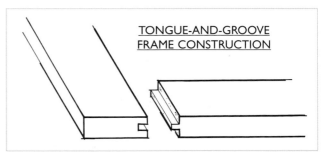

1–3. *Tongue-and-groove joint used in frame construction.*

that are now scrap wood. Even if you're only making one cabinet, that's *a lot* of setup time. Amateur woodworkers especially, with maybe two to four hours a week to work, don't have time to fool around with elaborate setups.

This leads to the final disadvantage of tongue-and-groove carcass joinery: figuring out measurements. If you have a 30-inch-wide cabinet, you need to cut the horizontal members to length taking into account how long the tongues will be. For a ⁵⁄₁₆-inch tongue, you need to add ⅝ inch to the total length of the piece—and take into account the less-than-¾-inch thickness of the plywood. For a 30-inch cabinet, that means a 28½-inch cross-member (30 inches minus 1½ inches—the plywood thickness), and the addition of ⅝ inch for the tongues, for a total of 29⅛ inches. The plywood isn't ¾ inch thick, so both side pieces together may measure 1⅞ or 1¹⁵⁄₃₂ inches instead of 1½ inches; you need to account for this. If the thickness of both vertical sides together measures 1¹⁵⁄₃₂ inches, for example, the cross-members won't be 29⅛ inches; they will instead be 29⁹⁄₃₂ inches. This is confusing enough when you're making one cabinet, much less 15 to 20 cabinets for a kitchen.

Oh, I almost forgot to mention clamps. Tongue-and-groove cabinet joinery also requires a lot of clamps, at least three top and bottom. You must somehow hold the large plywood pieces, wet with glue, in place while you put the clamps on, so it's better if you have two people.

▼ QUICK AND EASY METHOD

The Biscuit Joint

The heart of the method described in this book is the biscuit jointer. A biscuit jointer cuts a cir-

cular-saw kerf (slot) in the two pieces of wood to be joined. A football-shaped, compressed wood "biscuit" (also called a "plate") goes in the glued slots (use yellow or white glue), and the pieces are clamped together. The biscuit swells from the moisture of the glue, and the result is an incredibly strong joint—not quite as strong as a mortise-and-tenon, but almost. The biscuit joint could be called a "high-tech mortise-and-tenon."

The swelling of the biscuit locks the joint, and the glue bonds it. When done right, this joint is so strong that the only way to get it apart is to bang it loose with a steel hammer. It seems impossible that this should be so, but it is. In addition, because the biscuit is less than ⅛ inch thick, the joint is almost all shoulder (**1–4**). This means the carcass joint will not rack. Also, joints tend to go together square.

A top-notch biscuit jointer costs as much as a mid-range contractor's table saw. But very affordable biscuit jointers are now available which perform very well. The heart of the most sophisticated machines is the fence system,

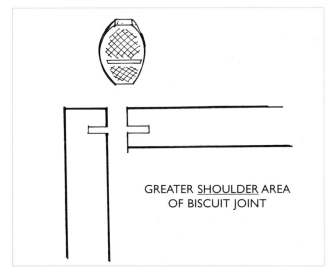

GREATER <u>SHOULDER</u> AREA
OF BISCUIT JOINT

1–4. The biscuit joint is almost all "shoulder." This is an advantage in that if the joint is used in carcass construction, it will not rack.

which can be adjusted very accurately and precisely, either at an angle or up and down. No matter—for the procedures I'll be describing, you don't even use the fence.

Clamping up is a necessity with biscuit joinery, but in this book only for the frame construction, in which case you use two clamps. For the large, cumbersome cabinet carcass, you won't use clamps at all. Screws are used to draw the vertical and horizontal members together, and since you put the carcass together in a *sequence* (lower right, top right, top left, lower left), it's an easy one-person job.

Machine setup is much easier also. You cut the pieces for one cabinet at a time, and then prepare them for joinery. It takes only five to ten minutes to cut all the biscuit slots and pilot holes for the screws. The biscuit jointer indexes to the pieces themselves **(1–5)**, so there are no machine setups that depend on other setups. This is a crucial point. It is why this procedure works so well and saves so much time. Nothing can go out of whack.

Measurements? These are greatly simplified. Since there are no tongues or grooves to allow for (and get confused over), all dimensions are absolute. For a 30-inch cabinet, you take the two vertical sides, measure them, and then subtract that measurement from 30. That's the measurement for the top and bottom pieces. If the plywood thickness is 23/32 inch (1/32 inch shy of the ¾-inch thickness), both sheets together measure 1⁷⁄₁₆ inches; 30 inches minus 1⁷⁄₁₆ inches equals 28⁹⁄₁₆ inches. Still too complicated? Use a storypole **(1–6)**. Make a mark for the total width of the carcass on a stick. When you make a mark for the thickness of the two sides, the distance from that part to the far end is the width of the horizontal member (top and bottom).

Can you use a storypole for the tongue-and-groove method? Yes, but you still must compen-

sate for the length of the tongues on each end of each horizontal member. And it's still confusing because you can accidentally cut to the shoulder mark instead of the total length mark—on one or both sides!

So this method really is quick and easy. You make one cabinet at a time, so there is no stockpiling of material. The shop is not tied up until you finish the dimensioning and joinery operations because there are no machine setups; you won't even need to adjust the fence on the biscuit jointer—you index the biscuit jointer to the materials! (more on this later). Measuring for sizes of cabinet parts is much simpler: total width minus the thickness of the sides. You don't need clamps to assemble the carcasses. Finally, the cost of the equipment is minimal— the major items you need are a table saw, biscuit jointer, and an electric drill.

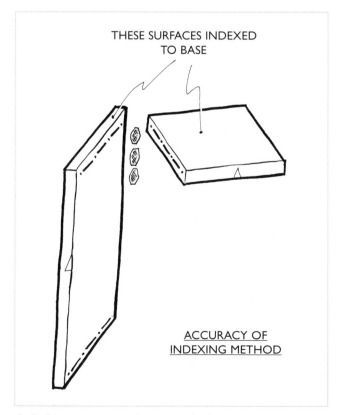

THESE SURFACES INDEXED
TO BASE

ACCURACY OF
INDEXING METHOD

1–5. Biscuit jointer indexing method.

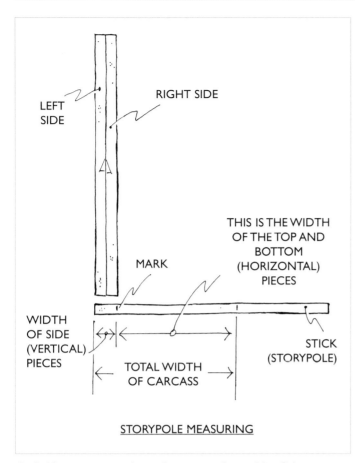

LEFT SIDE

RIGHT SIDE

THIS IS THE WIDTH OF THE TOP AND BOTTOM (HORIZONTAL) PIECES

MARK

WIDTH OF SIDE (VERTICAL) PIECES

STICK (STORYPOLE)

TOTAL WIDTH OF CARCASS

STORYPOLE MEASURING

1–6. Using a storypole to determine the width of the top and bottom pieces of a carcass. This is fast, accurate, and foolproof.

"Criticisms" of This Method

Believe it or not, people have told me that this method is too easy, too fast (woodworking shouldn't take so little effort!), and that it minimizes the skills that a proper craftsman needs to have—joint-cutting, measuring, etc. To a degree, that is true. Good woodworkers should all learn proper hand-tool skills, and should know the proper way to make all types of joints—whether by machine or by hand. There is no justifying a lack of skill in woodworking. And, too, for a cus-

1–7 (right). Wall cabinets made using the effective and simple cabinetmaking techniques discussed in the following chapters.

tomer willing to pay for them, or for your own personal work, traditional joinery methods are perfectly fine, of course.

On the other hand, as a one-person furniture/cabinetmaker, I could not make a profitable living without using the methods described in this book. Lots of very talented craftsmen are going broke by spending two hours cutting a joint that can be done just as well in five minutes. Woodworking—professional and otherwise—is very labor-intensive. Plus, it is very much a woodworking purist's dictum that the strongest and fastest joint for a given job is always the best joint. There is no merit in making things difficult. If biscuits and screws are just as strong and ten times faster, then they are the best choice.

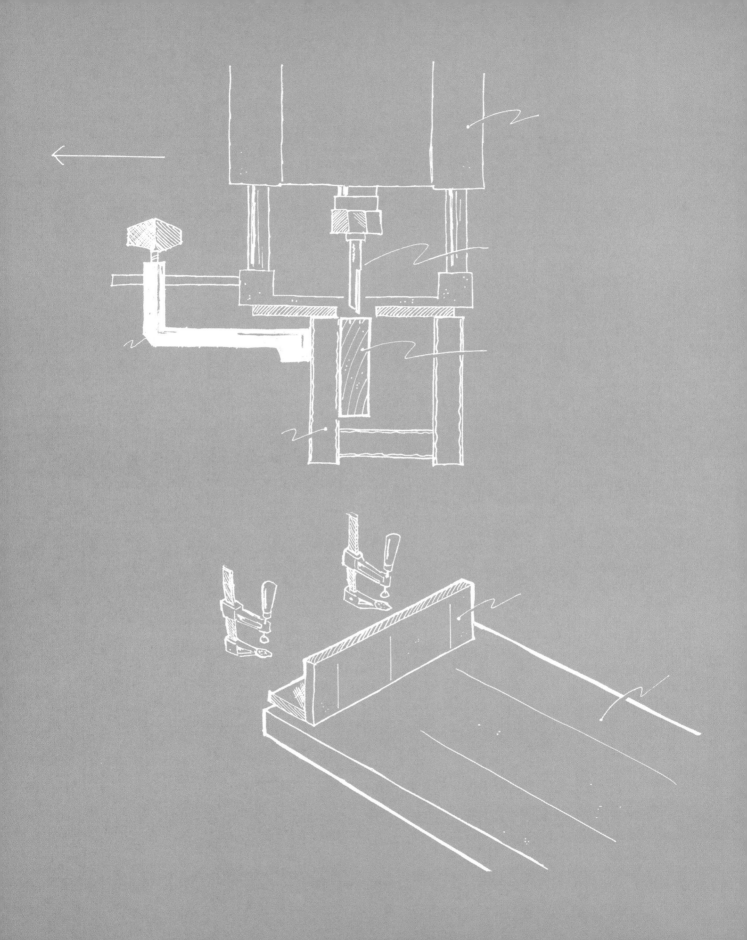

Tools and Accessories

Not many tools are required for this cabinet-making technique. You'll need a table saw to cut the pieces to the required dimensions; a biscuit jointer and electric drill to join them; a router to cut the rabbet for the cabinet backs and make the grooves in the frame-and-panel doors; a hand plane to smooth the edges of the solid-wood face frame and door parts; and a few other sundry hand tools. In addition to these tools, there are some necessary jigs and accessories you can easily make yourself.

What follows are guidelines based on my experience with these tools and information for making and using the jigs and accessories.

▼ POWER TOOLS

Table Saw

A table saw is necessary to accurately and quickly cut the cabinet and door parts to proper dimensions. Theoretically, you could use a handheld circular saw, but it's really much easier with a table saw.

There are many different types of table saw on the market today, but they usually all fall into one of three categories: cabinet saw, contractor's saw, and bench-top saw. As long as it has a miter-gauge slot and a reasonably accurate fence that goes to 24 inches, it will work.

Cabinet Saw

A cabinet saw (2–1) is a heavy saw with a large motor and massive castings that are all enclosed in a cabinet; hence the name. It runs quieter and is more vibration-free than the other types of table saw, and can handle heavy work for long periods. Some woodworkers claim it is also capable of greater accuracy. This is the saw I use, but only because I do a lot of work and like the quieter, more vibration-free operation. It is by no means essential.

Contractor's Saw

A contractor's saw (2–2) looks like a bench-top saw mounted on an integral stand. It has lighter castings and a smaller motor than the cabinet saw, but heavier and larger ones than the bench-top models. It is the type of table saw most woodworkers use, and works very well for all but the most heavy work (hours of sawing 8/4 oak or maple). There are belt-driven and direct-drive types available. Either one will work well; belt-driven designs may be a bit quieter.

Bench-Top Saw

This table saw (2–3) is the lightest and noisiest of the three saws. Usually these are direct-drive saws, and have aluminum tables, smaller fences, and miter gauges. One person can lift and carry a bench-top saw, so they are frequently used by better finish carpenters on the job site. For the cabinetmaking methods in this book, this type of table saw is perfectly adequate; just be sure it is clamped or bolted down securely.

Most woodworking writers and teachers tend to overcomplicate everything, especially equipment. The best woodworker I ever saw used an old Sears 8-inch table saw, built in 1950, and for 40 years did beautiful work with it. Whichever saw you use, work carefully and smart and you'll do fine work also.

TABLE SAW SAFETY GUIDELINES

Pay attention to the following guidelines when using a table saw:

✦ 1. Do not cut stock with knots, twists, or cupping. Cut only true stock that will not become pinched in the blade.

✦ 2. Use only sharp blades that are not coated with resin. Always keep the blade low (no more than ¼ inch higher than the stock thickness).

✦ 3. Control all cuts with a miter gauge, fence, or safety devices like push sticks and feather boards. Never attempt to cut freehand. This can cause the

stock to kick back. Always use the guard. (In the photos in this book, the guard on the table saw has been removed, for clarity. You, however, should always use the guard.)

✦ 4. Always wear safety glasses, ear protection, and gloves when using a table saw.

✦ 5. Protect yourself from dust by either using a dust-collection system with your table saw or a dust mask.

✦ 6. As with all power tools, do not work when distracted, tired, or under the influence of alcohol or medication.

✦ 7. When I use a table saw, I have everything I need in front of me, and once the blade is spinning I don't take my eyes off it until it stops. If you're always watching the blade, you are more likely to keep your hands away from it.

Saw Blades

Most of my table-saw work is done with 24- or 28-tooth, general-purpose saw blades. The ones shown in 2–4 are reasonably priced and work very well. I have experienced no tear-out on cabinet plywoods using these blades provided the "good" face is up as the sheet is fed through the saw. There is slight tear-out on the underside, but since this doesn't show, it's fine. If you wish to eliminate tear-out altogether, you can score the veneer with a sharp knife along the cut line.

I've found that a 40- or 50-tooth blade can help too in that it can slightly reduce tear-out. I have also used special-purpose triple-tooth-configuration blades to cut Formica-type materials, but find them unnecessary for plywoods.

Biscuit Jointer

The biscuit jointer is the primary tool for the method of cabinetmaking described in this

2–1. *A cabinet saw like this one has heavy castings and the most vibration-free operation of any American-designed saw.*

2–3. *This portable, light-duty bench-top saw is satisfactory for all the procedures described in this book.*

2–2. *This contractor's saw is somewhat lighter duty than the cabinet saw, and a good choice for cabinet work.*

2–4. *Twenty-four- or 28-tooth circular-saw blades are the standard-use saw blades in my shop.*

2–5. *A very inexpensive biscuit jointer with a simple fence system. (The photos in this book show biscuit jointers being used without their D-handles, for clarity. The D-handle should always be used.)*

2–6. *The fence on this biscuit jointer detaches from the machine for utilizing the methods in this book.*

2–7. *This machine has a rack-and-pinion adjustable fence and infinite angle adjustments between 45 and 90 degrees.*

2–8. *This biscuit jointer has a very sophisticated fence system, powerful motor, and a provision for a "face-frame"-sized biscuit (used with a special blade).*

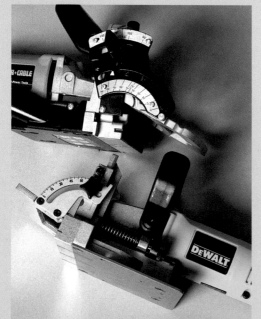

2–10. *This tool has the closest tolerances between the motor housing and sliding carriage, as well as a micro blade adjustment (visible at top). This is the most accurate biscuit jointer made.*

2–9. *Different angle settings are possible with these biscuit jointers.*

book. There are a variety of models available. The machine shown in **2–5** and **2–6** is a lower-priced model with a manually adjusted fence. It makes biscuit slots at 90 and 45 degrees only, but is quite adequate for the techniques described in this book.

The biscuit jointer shown in **2–7** has a rack-and-pinion adjustable fence and infinite angle adjustments between 45 and 90 degrees. For more involved applications, it can solve problems the model shown in **2–5** and **2–6** cannot.

The biscuit jointer shown in **2–8** and **2–9** has the most advanced fence system and the most powerful motor of all the models available. The fence can index from the outside of the workpiece when making angled cuts; this is a more accurate system for cabinetry work. This machine can also utilize a smaller blade for a special-size biscuit.

Illus. **2–10** shows the most accurate biscuit jointer made. The machining between the carriage and motor housing is superior to any other machine. It also has a "memory" system that can adjust the cutter up and down in microincrements. It has no rack-and-pinion fence.

BISCUIT JOINTER SAFETY GUIDELINES

Pay attention to these guidelines when using a biscuit jointer:

✦ 1. Keep biscuit-jointer cutters sharp and maintain them properly. Dull cutters are potentially dangerous.

✦ 2. Use the D-handle on the biscuit jointer. It is a valuable safety device. (In the photos in this book, the D-handle has been removed, for clarity. You, however, should always use the D-handle.)

✦ 3. Never attempt to adjust a biscuit jointer or other power tool while it is plugged in.

✦ 4. Wear proper safety equipment. These include safety goggles or glasses and hearing and dust protection.

Electric Drill

Almost everyone on earth owns an electric drill, and as long as it has variable speed and reverses, it's fine. I use a ⅜-inch model. A ½-inch type will work as well, but may be a bit heavy. The ⅜-inch electric drill shown in **2–11** is a good choice: it's not too large, has plenty of power, and is very comfortable to position and maneuver. It's a quality tool that will last a long time.

Cordless Drills

Small cordless drills like the ones shown in **2–12** are quite a luxury. The 9.6-volt Hitachi and DeWalt models shown don't have the power of the larger Porter Cable cordless drill, but they are so small and lightweight you can get them into awkward spots inside cabinets for installing mounting rails, etc.

I like to use a quick-change drill/countersink/driver system in my drill when making cabinets. These units mount in the drill chuck and allow you to quickly change from drill bits and countersinks to a screwdriver bit. Two very effective types are shown in **2–13** and **2–14**. These save considerable time.

Angle (Close-Quarter) Drills

Angle drills (**2–15** and **2–16**) are a great convenience for a cabinetmaker. These drills can fit into a very tight spot, like a drawer opening, where a pistol-handle drill will not. They are available from several manufacturers in corded and cordless models. The one on the right in **2–15** is a switch-activated variable-speed model, most useful for driving screws.

2–11. A ³/₈-inch electric drill. A simple electric drill like this one is good for pilot-hole drilling and driving in screws.

2–12. Cordless drills like these, while not essential, are a great convenience.

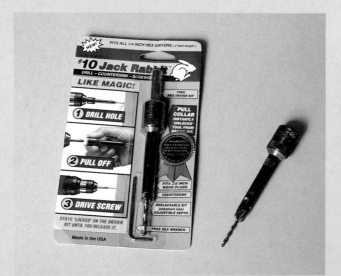

2–13. This drill accessory makes it fast work to change from drilling/countersinking to drilling in screws.

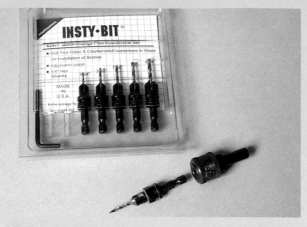

2–14. This drill accessory comes with a quick-change chuck, and a number of different-sized drills and countersinks can be interchanged.

2–15. Angle or close-quarter drills. The two at the left are corded; the one on the right is cordless. This switch-activated variable-speed model is most useful for driving screws in tight areas. For drilling and countersinking, any model should work well.

2–16. Angle drill in use. Even with a full-sized drill bit in place, the drill easily fits into a very small drawer opening. Here I'm drilling for a side guide.

ELECTRIC DRILL SAFETY GUIDELINES

Pay attention to these guidelines when using an electric drill:

+ 1. Wear safety glasses and other appropriate safety equipment for all jobs performed with the electric drill.
+ 2. Chuck bits securely with the power disconnected.
+ 3. Remove the chuck key after installing the bit.
+ 4. Do not force the bit.

Router

A fixed-base router is necessary to rabbet the backs of cabinets to receive a plywood back. The D-handle design **(2–17)** is the most comfortable. You'll need a ⅜-inch rabbeting bit **(2–18)**. Use a carbide or carbide-tipped bit because it cuts better. Also, a ½-inch shank is preferable to a ¼-inch one. I also like to use a ⅛-inch round-over bit **(2–19)** to break the sharp edges on face frames, doors, and carcasses, although this is easily done with the orbital sander.

A plunge router **(2–20)** is needed for making the grooves in door rails and stiles to receive a plywood panel. Doing this work with a fixed-base router is difficult. A ¼-inch straight-cutting or spiral bit **(2–21)** will work. A ¼-inch spiral bit is only available with a ¼-inch shank.

Lots of craftsmen don't put backs on cabinets. The thinking is, the unit mounts against the wall anyway, so what's the point? If that's you, you don't need the rabbeting bit. In addition to this, if you plan on having solid doors as opposed to frame-and-panel doors, you don't need the straight-cutting bit. If you're making cabinets with no backs and solid-wood doors, you don't need a router.

2–17. *This D-handle router has a powerful motor and is very easy to hold upright and control.*

2–18. *A ³/8-inch rabbeting bit with a pilot bearing is used to make the rabbet in the back of the cabinet.*

2–19. A ⅛-inch round-over bit. Using the lower edge of this bit allows a very subtle treatment to sharp edges of face-frame and door materials. The more common ¼-inch type leaves too large a radius.

2–20. A plunge router is needed to rout the grooves in the frame-and-panel rails and stiles.

2–21. Straight flute and spiral upcut bits can be used to rout the ¼-inch groove.

ROUTER SAFETY GUIDELINES

Pay attention to the following guidelines when using a router:

✦ 1. Make sure the switch is off before plugging the router in or touching it.

✦ 2. Always unplug the router when changing bits and bases, servicing the router, or adjusting accessories.

✦ 3. Make sure the bits are clean, sharp, properly installed, and firmly tightened in the collet.

✦ 4. Clamp the workpiece securely to a bench or table.

✦ 5. Feed the router against the bit's rotation.

✦ 6. If the switch on the router is located such that you have to reach for it or remove your grip from the router table or knob, you may want to use a foot-switch accessory.

✦ 7. Wear the proper safety equipment (glasses or goggles, hearing protection, and dust masks) and, if possible, use a dust-collection system.

Orbital Sander

An orbital sander **(2–22)** has a square pad that takes sandpaper and moves in a tiny circular pattern (orbit) to smooth surfaces. It is also very useful for rounding over sharp edges on face frames and doors. For those who can only afford one sander, an orbital sander is the type to have. The square pad can get into corners, the sander is easy to control even on edge, and, if kept in constant motion, it will not leave swirl marks.

Orbital sanders are finishing sanders—they can be used with 80-grit and finer (100, 120, 150, 220, etc.) sandpaper. Better-quality orbital sanders will not leave you feeling like you've just vibrated your hands and arms off.

Belt Sander

The belt sander is good for removing lots of material quickly, as well as for smoothing or shaping edges of doors or face frames. The sanders shown in **2–23** are 3 × 21-inch models, which is a good size for cabinetmaking work.

SANDER SAFETY GUIDELINES

Pay attention to the following guidelines when using a sander:

✦ 1. Always use the guard when operating the sander.
✦ 2. Do not operate machines with torn or ripped belts or discs.
✦ 3. Always attempt to place your work against the rest on the sander.
✦ 4. On the horizontal belt sander, always sand so that the belt motion is away from you.

▼ HAND TOOLS
Hand Plane

You'll need a hand plane to shave off the saw marks left from the table saw on solid wood, usually on the edges. It may also help straighten them a bit. It can also be used to flatten any surface irregularities where the stiles and rails join. I would use a jack plane (about 15 inches)

2–22. *Useful for all types of finish sanding, this orbital sander uses sandpaper from 80 grit on upward. Power, low vibration, and aggressive action are the strong points of this unit.*

2–23. *Both of these belt sanders take belts 3 inches wide x 21 inches long, are powerful, and can be easily maneuvered.*

2–24. Wooden and metal jack planes.

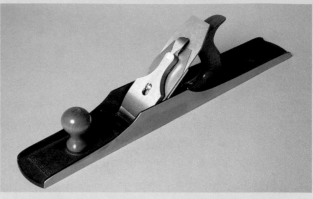
2–25. A metal jointer plane, about 22 inches long.

2–26. Dovetail or "gents" saws.

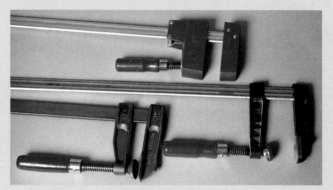
2–27. Good clamps such as these are a pleasure to use when building cabinets.

(2–24) or a jointer plane (which is longer—about 22 inches) (2–25). Almost any hand plane will work as long as the cap iron fits tight to the blade and the blade is razor-sharp. If you're buying one, get a better-quality plane—it'll be easier to set up. A sharp blade, however, solves 90 percent of planing difficulties.

A belt sander can also be used to remove saw marks. No, don't use the orbital sander to do this—it takes too long and doesn't leave a crisp edge. Of course, if you have a power jointer, you can use that to remove the saw marks, but then you'll need to sand—or plane off—the jointer marks!

Handsaw

A simple "gents" or "dovetail" saw (2–26) is necessary to trim biscuits on face frames and frame-and-panel doors. These have turned handles and are very small and inexpensive.

Clamps

Good clamps (2–27) are a pleasure to use and work well all the time. Poor-quality clamps have rough operating movements and twist out of alignment as you tighten them—an avoidable nuisance.

Chisels

Every woodworker needs a good set of chisels. A high-quality set of plastic-(cellulose-acetate-) handled butt chisels is helpful to have for occasionally trimming a biscuit or plug, squaring up the rabbets in the cabinet back, and trimming a groove. If you eventually want to use leaf hinges for flush-fit doors, you'll have chisels to cut the mortises.

The chisels shown in **2–28** have a metal striking cap atop the plastic handle, which is very nice if you drive the chisels with a steel carpenter's hammer. The handles are comfort-

able, and the size is just right—you can get your hands close to the work. The blades are carbon steel and take a nice, razor-sharp edge.

The wood-handle chisels shown in **2–29** are comfortable to hold and are made to be tapped using a wooden mallet. More traditional looking than the plastic-handled chisels, these tools also will take a sharp edge.

Japanese chisels **(2–30)** have the most durable cutting edges, although they require a bit of fussing with the handle and hoop and sharpening with water stones. These are best tapped with a Japanese steel hammer **(2–31)**.

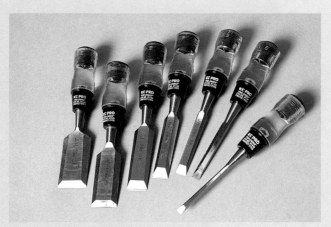

2–28. *A set of rugged, plastic-handled butt chisels with good steel blades.*

2–29. *Short-bladed chisels with wood handles.*

2–30. *Japanese chisels. Laminated steel chisels have the longest-lasting edge.*

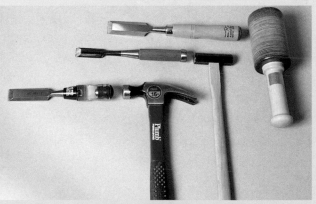

2–31. *Striking tools. Plastic-handle chisels can be struck with a steel carpenter's hammer (bottom). Japanese chisels are best struck with a Japanese steel hammer (center), and wood-handle chisels with a wooden mallet.*

Hammer

An ordinary carpenter's hammer **(2–32)** is all you'll need for nailing plywood backs to cabinets, tapping chisels, and for an occasional gentle blow to get a cabinet side flush. Have a nail set handy also.

Balance is the big issue with carpenter's hammers. I've used pricey high-tech graphite and jacketed hammers that have such poor balance they are like swinging a brick. Some of the better all-steel and fiberglass-handle types have very good balance and are much easier to use. Japanese hammers also have very good balance.

Additional Tools and Equipment

The following tools and equipment will be needed when building cabinets:

1. *Tape Measure.* A 12- or 16-foot tape measure **(2–33** and **2–34)** is a good size for making cabinets.

2. *Wood Rule.* A 36-inch English-style wooden rule **(2–34)** doesn't bend and flex, so it's handy for measuring parts and components at the workbench.

3. *Combination Square.* This tool is very versatile. The one shown in **2–34** is the most accurate.

4. *Glue Bottles.* Once you use a glue bottle **(2–35)**, it will be difficult to do without one. It will precisely coat the biscuit slot with glue.

5. *Glue.* I find plain old white glue **(2–36)** the best all-around woodworking glue. It dries clear and has a longer setup time. When hardened, the excess is more rubbery—which makes it easier to scrape or slice off.

2–32. Right: Japanese hammer with wood handle. Center: Hammer with steel handle. Left: Hammer with fiberglass handle.

2–33. This tape measure allows for very easy reading.

2–34. Measuring tools. Clockwise from top: 12-inch combination square, tape measure, pencil, marking knife, and wooden folding rule.

2–35 (left). These glue bottles greatly aid assembly of biscuit-joined members. 2–36 (right). White glue is the best all-around woodworking glue.

▼ SHOP-MADE ACCESSORIES

Here are a few accessories to make your cabinetmaking life easier. They are also very useful for other woodworking applications. You can make them from scrap.

Clamping Stands

Clamping stands (**2–37**) are made from two pieces of 5 inch or wider, ¾-inch-thick plywood scrap, screwed and glued together at a 90-degree angle in a "T" shape. Slightly round over the tops with an orbital sander. They can be from 24 to 30 inches in length. Make them in pairs. These are great for laying face frames or doors on while clamping. Not only do they ensure that the piece will dry flat, but by "hanging" the clamps off the bottom of the piece it's easy to check the diagonals for square. I once glued up (flat!) a 38 × 84-inch radius-top storm door with two large clamping stands.

Panel-Cutting Jig

Panel cutters are extremely useful in cabinetwork. I like this panel-cutting jig (**2–38**) because it prevents the blade from dangerously emerg-

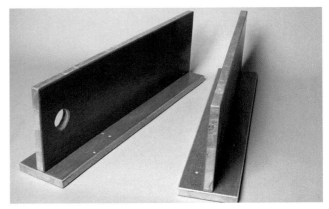

2–37. *A pair of wooden clamping stands.*

ing from a hidden position under the jig. It's compact, very accurate, and easy to make (**2–39**). Take a 20-inch strip of hardwood—oak, hard maple, etc.—and dimension it to fit in the miter-gauge slot in the table saw, flush with the top (**2–40**). Place the piece in the left-side slot in your table saw and run a bead of glue over the top (**2–41**). Place the ¾-inch piece of plywood on top, butted to the blade, and screw the plywood to the strip (**2–42** and **2–43**). If you don't assemble this on the table saw, it won't slide smoothly. Install a dowel at the end of this for a pull-back handle.

Now the fence—a 2 × 29-inch strip of straight hardwood or plywood screwed, not glued, to the top of the plywood piece. Install one screw on the right end of the fence. With a rafter square, square the fence to the saw blade plate, not the

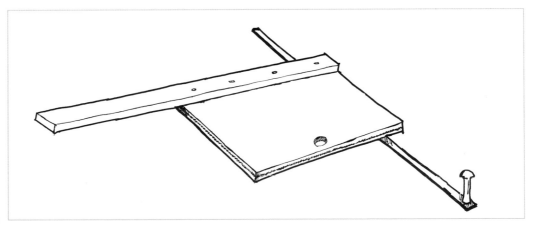

2–38. *Panel-cutting jig.*

teeth, and secure the fence at the left side with another screw (**2–44**).

Next, take a test panel of plywood, Masonite, etc., that's at least 15 x 20 inches and crosscut one of the ends with the panel cutter. Flip it end for end—the same edge to the fence—and cut the other side (**2–45**). Turn off the saw and measure the diagonals (corner to corner) (**2–46**).

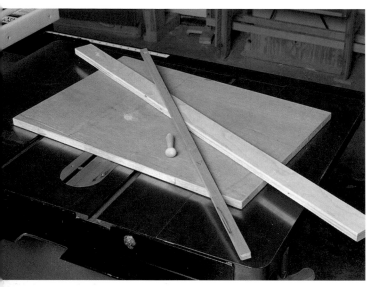

2–39. Materials for making a panel-cutting jig.

2–40. Fitting the hardwood strip in the table saw's miter-gauge slot.

2–41. Applying a bead of white glue to the hardwood strip in the miter-gauge slot.

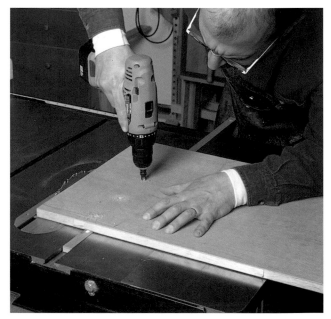

2–42. Making pilot holes in plywood and hardwood strips.

If they are equal (within 1/32 inch), the jig is fine, so screw the fence down with a few more screws. If not, adjust it, screwing the fence down in a different spot and retesting, until the diagonals are equal. The reason we test the jig by measuring diagonals on a test panel is because that's what the panel cutter is actually used for—cutting panels accurately.

2–43. *Screwing the plywood to the hardwood strip.*

2–44. *Screwing the fence to the plywood.*

2–45. *Test-cutting a panel.*

2–46. *Measuring the diagonals of the test panel. Note that the saw is shut off and the blade is completely retracted.*

Stop Block

The stop block (**2–47**) is used in conjunction with the panel cutter. A small leaf hinge (about one inch) connects a small block to a longer piece that can clamp to the fence. With the block in the "down" position, measure over from the saw blade to the block and clamp the other end to the fence. To use it, flip the small

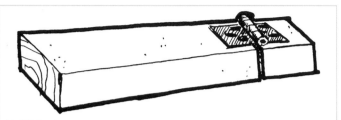

2–47. Stop block.

piece up and butt one end of the piece you're cutting to the remaining end (**2–48**). Make your cut (**2–49**). Move the small block to the down position, flip the piece end for end like the test panel (**2–50**), and make the second cut (**2–51**). Both ends will be cut square, and you can easily make repeatable cuts for things like cabinet face frame and door parts. This procedure is shown in the following chapters.

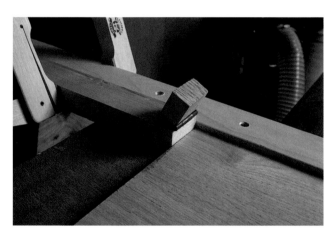

2–48 to **2–51.** Using a stop block. Here the stop block is in the open position with material butted to it.

2–49. Making the first cut. The stop block is in the open position. This gets the first edge accurately square.

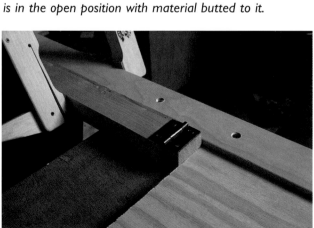

2–50. The stop block in the closed position. The material has been flipped—the freshly cut edge is now butted to the block. The same edge is against the fence.

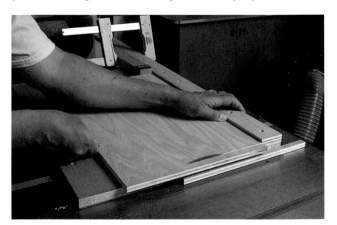

2–51. Making the final cut. This squares up the entire panel and cuts it to final length. Note that the stop block is in the closed position.

Squaring Blocks

A squaring block (**2–52**) is a 90-degree corner made of 5 x 5-inch or larger pieces of plywood. They are spring-clamped onto the insides of cabinets to keep them square while they dry.

Screw and glue together the parts as shown in **2–53**. I use a good-quality combination square to be sure the angle is precisely 90 degrees. If the blocks aren't at 90 degrees, they are of no use, obviously.

Router Jig

With this jig*, you can accurately rout grooves in rails and stiles for frame-and-panel doors. The jig is "U"-shaped (**2–54**). Make it a little longer than the longest rail or stile you'll have to rout—mine is about 36 inches. Making the inside span of the U three inches will accommodate a router with a six-inch base. The vertical members of the U should be below the base about ¼ inch so the jig will be flat when clamped in bench dogs. You can also clamp it in an English-style vise.

Vertical members should be four inches up from the base and at 90 degrees to it, parallel to

2–53. Squaring blocks and spring clamps.

each other, and exactly the same height. Glue and screw the jig together.

In use, the rail or stile is clamped in the near-side of the U, flush with the top. The router's edge guide bears along the outside of the same edge. I mark the ¼-inch groove width in one of the door parts and adjust the router edge guide until the bit is aligned with the mark (**2–55**).

You only need to mark one piece—all the others will be routed identically. Index the

*A router jig is also referred to as a mortise jig.

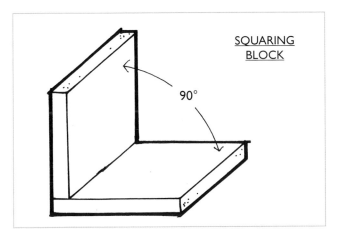

2–52. A squaring block is a 90-degree plywood corner that is clamped onto the insides of cabinets to keep them square while they dry.

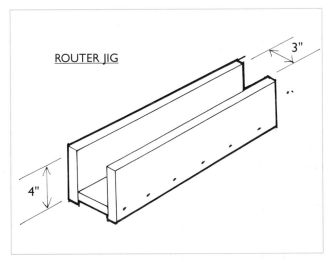

2–54. Router jig.

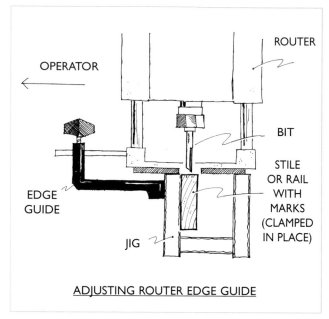

ROUTER

OPERATOR

BIT

EDGE
GUIDE

STILE
OR RAIL
WITH
MARKS
(CLAMPED
IN PLACE)

JIG

ADJUSTING ROUTER EDGE GUIDE

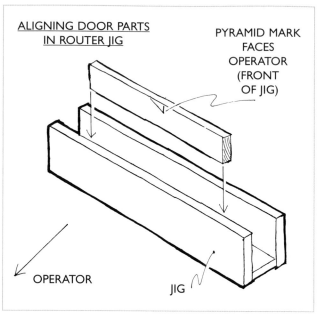

ALIGNING DOOR PARTS
IN ROUTER JIG

PYRAMID MARK
FACES
OPERATOR
(FRONT
OF JIG)

OPERATOR

JIG

2–55. *With the rail or stile clamped in the jig, the edge guide is adjusted until the bit is aligned with the two marks.*

2–56. *If the door member is always oriented in the jig with the pyramid mark facing the operator, the grooves will always align when the door is assembled.*

front face of the door parts (the side with the pyramid) toward you (**2–56**); then if the groove isn't perfectly centered, all the grooves will line up when the door is assembled. If the clamps get in the way of the router, the door parts can be held in the jig with wedges.

Bench Stop

The bench stop (**2–57**) is a 90-degree form made of plywood, with indexing lines drawn on it. It is clamped to the end of the bench and is used to accurately index the biscuit jointer to the cabinet parts **(2–58)**.

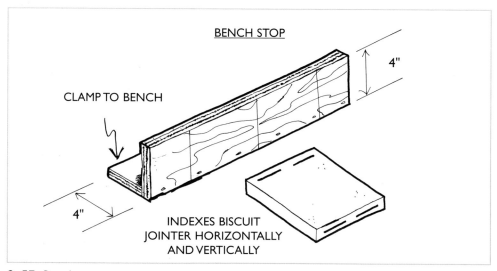

BENCH STOP

4"

CLAMP TO BENCH

4"

INDEXES BISCUIT
JOINTER HORIZONTALLY
AND VERTICALLY

2–57. *Bench stop.*

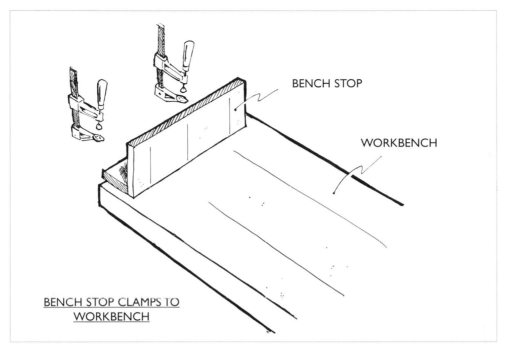

2–58. Clamped to the workbench, the bench stop assists with aligning parts for biscuiting.

▼ CABINET HARDWARE

Hinges

For the cabinet method shown in this book, we will be using ⅜-inch *overlap hinges*—(**2–59**). Using this hinge exclusively will simplify the cabinetmaking process, initially. The overlap design is very forgiving, self-closing, and nice-looking. Don't buy hinges in home centers; they are invariably of very poor quality. Use a cabinetmaking supplier or a woodworking supply catalog. Once you are confident with this hinge, you can move on to using other types, of course.

Knobs

I prefer very simple-looking knobs made of wood. The types with a round tenon hold more securely than the screw-in types (**2–60**).

With these tools and accessories, you'll have what you need to make cabinets.

2–59. Three-eighth-inch overlap hinges.

2–60. Cabinet knobs. The two at left have tenons; the one at right uses a screw.

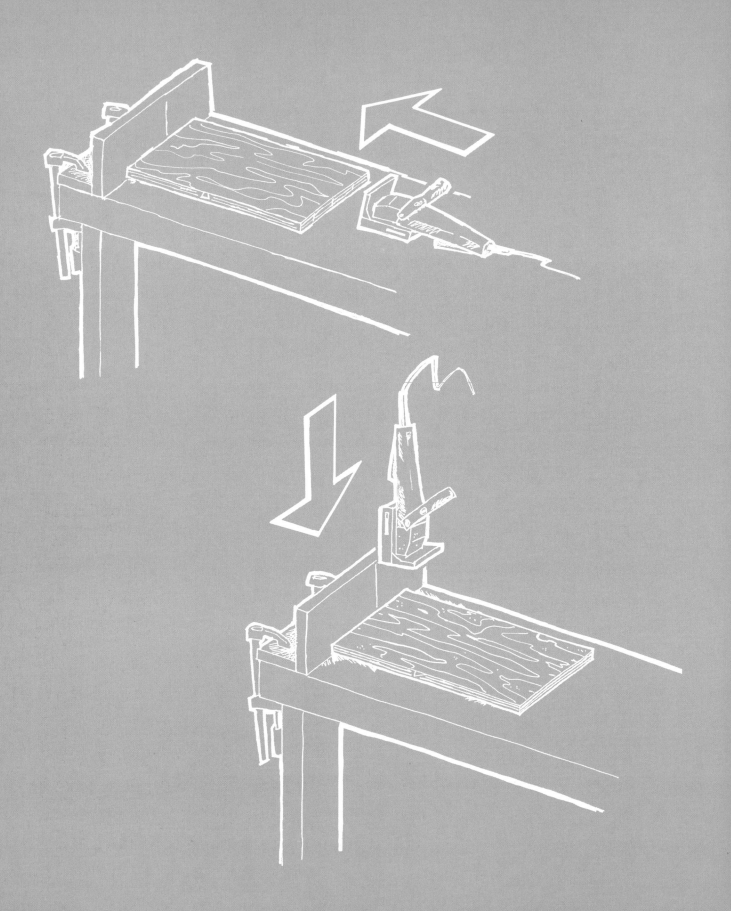

CHAPTER
3

Biscuit-Jointing and Assembling Carcasses and Face Frames

The method of building cabinets discussed in this book involves biscuit-jointing cabinet members together, both carcass and face-frame parts (**3–1**). The carcass parts are not clamped; they are screwed together to secure the biscuit joints. This allows for very easy assembly of the big pieces. The frame parts do need to be clamped together, but with two or three clamps per frame and the whole thing done on the clamping stands, it's easy. The biscuit-jointing of carcass and frame parts is described below.

3–1. This "roll around" cabinet was built by biscuit-jointing the carcass.

▼ CARCASS JOINTS

Biscuit Slots

I am illustrating the technique using two 12-inch-wide pieces of ¾-inch-thick cabinet-grade plywood. They are simulated bottom and left-side cabinet pieces (**3–2**). The pyramid marking system, which is described in Chapter 5, has been used on them. We are going to cut biscuit slots, drill and countersink, and drill again for pilot holes.

In cabinet construction, the side pieces run the full length of the carcass; therefore, the slots are cut on the edges of the top and bottom pieces (**3–3**) and on the *inside faces* (flat part) of the side pieces (**3–4**).

Mark the biscuit positions on a stick. The stick should be about 14 inches long—not less than 12 inches. Write "front" on the end; then with a ruler make marks 2, 5½, and 9 inches from the front (**3–5**). You will mark the pieces with this stick. Why use this stick instead of a tape meas-

3–2. *Simulated carcass pieces, used to demonstrate my method of cabinetmaking.*

ure? Because it's more accurate. By not having to transfer marks from a ruler on each piece, nothing can be marked wrong. (The first rule of measuring accurately is to not measure at all if you can help it.)

When using the stick on the side (vertical) piece, hold the "front" of the stick with the front

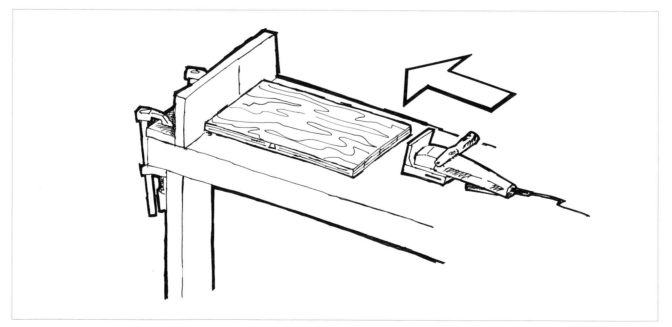

3–3. *Biscuiting carcass tops and bottoms.*

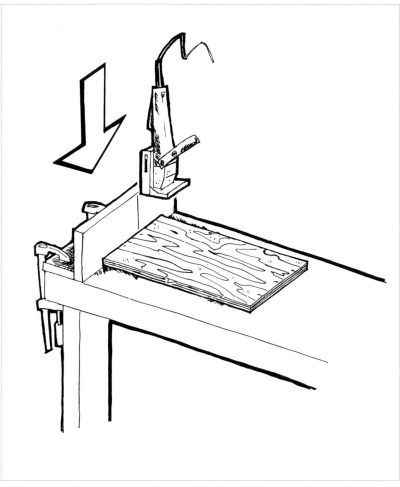

3–4. Biscuiting carcass sides.

3–5. Marking biscuit positions on a stick. This eliminates errors resulting from taking repeated measurements.

of the piece; that is, where the pyramid mark is. (Illus. **5–12**, on page 89, shows the pyramid marking system for a face-frame assembly.) Transfer the marks from the stick to the lower inside face of the workpiece (**3–6**). On the bottom (horizontal) piece do the same,

3–6. Using the stick to transfer the marks to the workpiece.

3–7. Transferring marks to the bottom piece. Notice that the mark is made on the edge of the piece.

except transfer the mark to the edge of the piece (**3–7**). The biscuit slots are now marked.

Position the bottom piece flat on the workbench, against the bench stop, with the pyramid

3–8. Bottom piece placed flat on workbench, butted to the bench stop.

3–9. Making biscuit cuts, with the biscuit jointer indexed to the marks on the piece.

mark up (**3–8**). (Making and using a bench stop is described in Chapter 2.) With the base of the biscuit jointer resting on the workbench, cut the three biscuit slots, aligning the index mark on the biscuit jointer with the pencil marks on the workpiece (**3–9**).

Next, take the side piece and lay it against the bench stop so that the lower inside face is against it and facing up. Line up one of the marks on the workpiece with the line on the bench stop (**3–10**). Hold the biscuit jointer vertically, with the index mark on the fence aligned with the same line on the bench stop. You'll need to sight down between the bottom of the biscuit jointer and the bench stop (**3–11**). Be sure the workpiece is tight to the bench stop when you plunge the blade. Make the cut (**3–12**). Repeat this for the other two marks (**3–13**).

Drilling Holes for Screws

I use the quick-change countersink accessory (refer to **2–14**) with a 1/8-inch bit to drill and countersink the holes in the side pieces. Whichever drill accessory you are using, set and lock the bit so that it extends beyond the countersink about one inch (**3–14**). Use a spring clamp to attach a backer board (a scrap piece) to the outside of the piece opposite the biscuit slots (**3–15**). This will prevent tear-out on the other side of the plywood when you drill.

3–10. Lining up one of the marks on the side piece with the mark on the bench stop.

3–13. All the biscuit slots cut in the side piece.

3–11. Sighting down the bottom of the biscuit jointer to align it to the index mark on the bench stop.

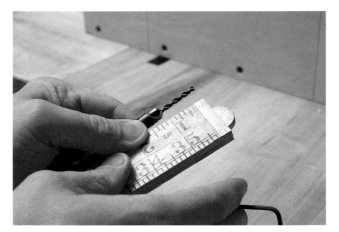

3–14. Setting the drill in the countersink accessory to one inch.

3–12. Cutting the biscuit slots in the side piece.

3–15. Attaching a backer board to the side piece with a spring clamp to prevent tear-out.

3–16. *Drilling holes adjacent to the biscuit slots.*

3–17. *Countersinking the holes, with the backer board removed.*

3–18. *The holes countersunk.*

Drill four holes in line with the biscuit slots, about ¼ inch to each side of them, from the inside out (**3–16**). Remove the backer board, turn the piece over, and countersink all the holes ⅜ inch (**3–17** and **3–18**). Next, assemble the pieces dry, with biscuits in place. Clamp this assembly together to a squaring block with spring clamps. Be sure the fronts of the pieces are flush (**3–19**).

Install a ⁷⁄₆₄-inch twist bit in the drill chuck, extended out to about two inches (**3–20**). Drill through the existing countersink and pilot holes to create a smaller pilot hole in the bottom piece (**3–21**). Do this carefully, clearing the flutes of the bit as you go and keeping the bit straight. Skinny bits like this can break easily. When all the pilot holes are drilled, you can assemble the pieces.

Assembly

In this last step, the slots and biscuits are glued, the pieces are put together and screwed, and the screw holes are plugged.

With one of the glue bottles shown in **2–35**, you can quickly put just the right amount of glue in each slot every time. An alternate approach is to squirt glue into the slot with a regular glue bottle and try to spread it evenly with an acid brush, but I find this unsatisfactory. There always seems to be either too much or too little glue in the slot, and it's time-consuming.

Whichever method you use, spread glue in the slots and on the biscuits (**3–22** and **3–23**). Coat the biscuits evenly (**3–24**). Put the two pieces together, holding them in position with the spring clamps and squaring blocks like before.

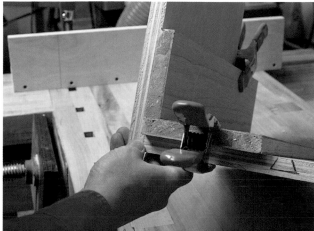

3–19. *The pieces dry-assembled and clamped together to a squaring block.*

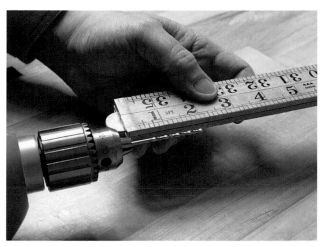

3–20. *The twist bit in the drill and extended two inches.*

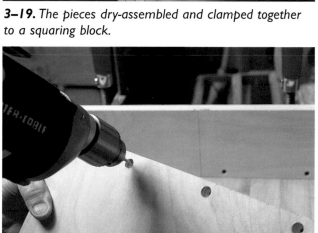

3–21. *Drilling through to create a smaller pilot hole in the bottom (horizontal) piece.*

3–22. *Applying glue to the side-piece biscuit slots.*

3–23. *Applying glue to the bottom-piece biscuit slots.*

3–24. *Spreading glue on a biscuit.*

3–25. Driving in drywall screws to pull the pieces together. The pieces are aligned and clamped with a squaring block.

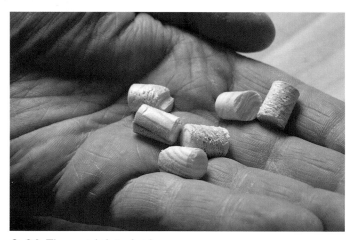

3–26. Three-eighth-inch plugs.

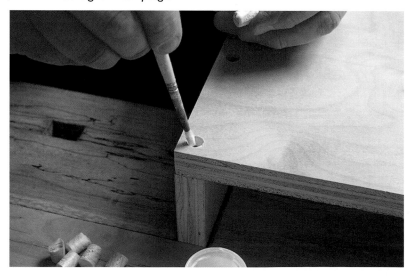

3–27. Applying glue to the countersink hole.

With the fronts of the pieces flush, drive in four 1⅝-inch drywall screws to pull the pieces together (**3–25**).

The countersink holes are then plugged. I cut plugs with a tapered plug cutter in a drill press. You can also buy plugs (**3–26**). Dab a little white glue in the hole (**3–27**) and on the plug (**3–28**). Place the plug in the hole and lightly tap it in with a hammer (**3–29**). With a chisel, trim the plug a little proud of the cabinet (**3–30**); then you can sand it flush with the orbital sander (**3–31**).

▼ FRAME JOINTS

Biscuit Slots

A frame joint, in cabinet design, is used on face and door frames. These were traditionally made with a mortise-and-tenon joint, but the biscuit joint is much faster and more than strong enough.

Since we are using 2¼-inch-wide x ¾-inch-thick stock for the cabinet in Part Two, let's use those same dimensions here. Use any solid hardwood that is convenient (poplar is a good choice) (**3–32**).

3–28. Applying glue to the plug.

3–29. Tapping in the plug with a hammer.

-30. Trimming the plug with a chisel.

3–31. Sanding the plug down flush with the orbital sander.

3–32. Two pieces of simulated frame pieces, each of poplar.

Using the pyramid system, mark one piece as the bottom and one as the left side (**3–33**). Draw a line on the side piece showing the width of the bottom piece (**3–34** and **3–35**). Now measure one inch from the bottom of the side piece and make a mark (**3–36**). Hold the bottom piece in position and transfer the mark to this piece (**3–37**). These are the marks to index the biscuit jointer from. A #20 biscuit will extend beyond the pieces at assembly, and be trimmed later; this will produce a clean inside edge.

Why have a visible joint show when there are smaller face-frame biscuits available that won't show? This is a valid question. Introducing dif-

3–33. Marking the pieces with pyramids.

3–35. The piece marked.

3–34. Drawing a line to mark the width of the bottom piece.

3–36. Making a mark one inch up from the bottom of the piece.

3–37. Transferring the mark to the other (bottom) piece.

3–39. Positioning the side piece against the stop block.

3–38. A protruding biscuit, neatly sawn and trimmed, is not objectionable to see.

3–40. Biscuit jointer in position to cut the slot.

ferent-sized biscuits and cutters complicates the method unnecessarily. Also, a visible biscuit, neatly trimmed and planed or sanded, isn't objectionable. I like the idea of the craftsman's method showing a bit. Trimmed biscuits are clearly seen on my built-in bathroom cabinets (**3–38**), and look fine.

Position the side piece against the stop block with the pyramid mark up and facing outward (**3–39**). (Stop blocks are described in Chapter 2.) Line up the biscuit jointer with the mark and cut the slot (**3–40**). Be sure the piece is flat against the workbench when you cut it. The cutter will emerge from the end of the workpiece, so keep your hands away.

When cutting the slot in the bottom piece,

you will be cutting into end grain. End grain is very hard. The biscuit jointer has a tendency to jump to one side as you make the cut, so it's a good idea to clamp the piece down (**3–41**). With the pyramid mark up, line up the biscuit jointer with the mark. Hold the machine down on the bench with one hand as you plunge the cutter into the piece with the other (**3–42**).

Assembling the Frame Pieces and Trimming the Biscuits

To assemble the frame pieces, spread glue in the slots and on the biscuits as before and hold the pieces tight together with a clamp (**3–43**). When we make the actual face and door frames for the cabinet, they'll be clamped up on stands. For now, I'll just clamp the two pieces together.

3–41. Clamping the bottom (end-grain) piece down.

3–43. Clamping the pieces together.

3–42. Making a biscuit cut in the end grain.

3–44. Sawing off the excess biscuit.

3–45. Planing the edges smooth.

3–46. Sanding the face members smooth.

When the glue is set (this takes about two hours), I trim off the excess biscuit with a small handsaw (**3–44**) and then plane or lightly belt-sand the edges smooth (**3–45**). If the front faces of the joined pieces aren't exactly flush, they can be planed until they are. They can also be sanded down with 80-grit sandpaper in the orbital sander (**3–46**). We don't use a belt sander here—it would leave scratches on the cross-grain piece. If you use a Lamello biscuit jointer, all other things being equal, the faces of each piece will always line up.

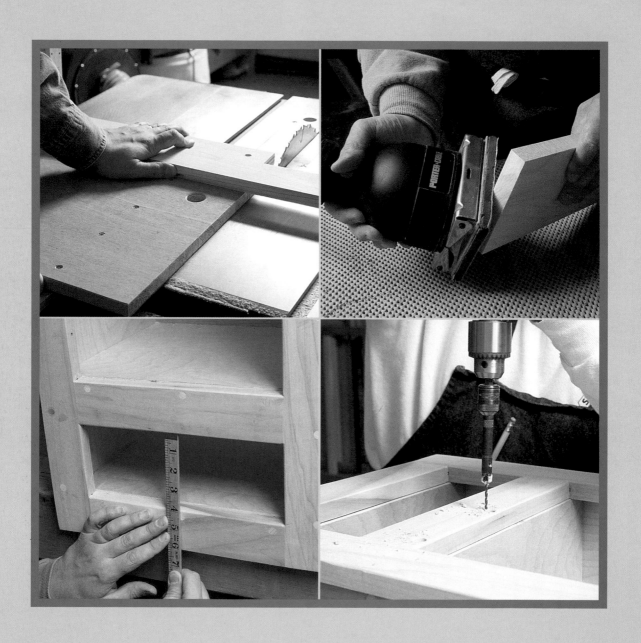

PART TWO

▼

Building a Cabinet
Step by Step

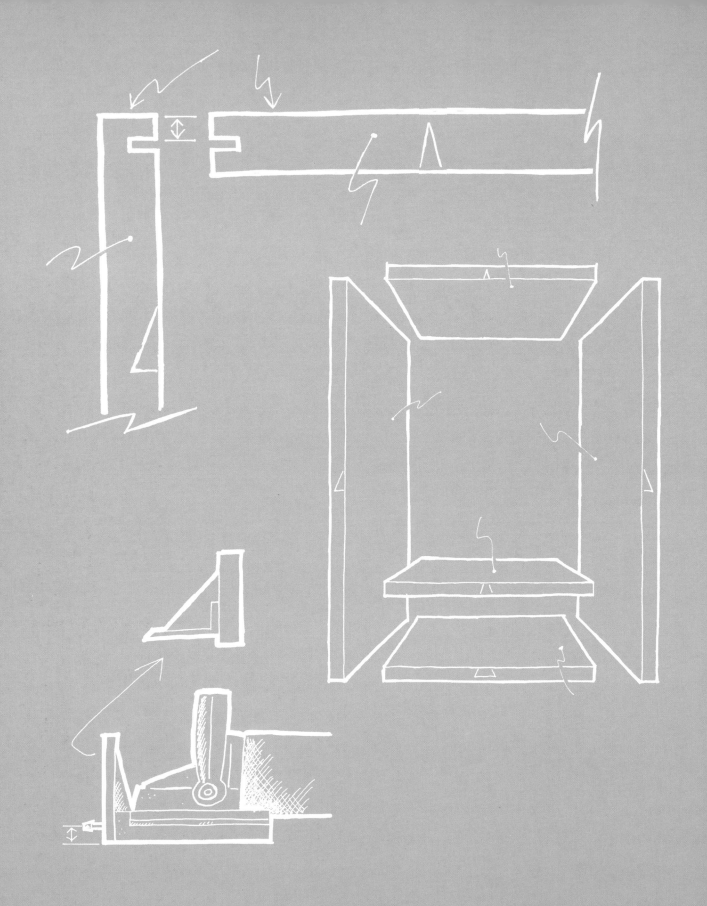

CHAPTER
4

Building The Carcass

▼ MATERIALS

Cabinet carcasses are best made from plywood—specifically hardwood-veneer plywood, which is a *cabinet-grade* material. Plywood is a good material, for several reasons. It is a dimensionally stable product. It doesn't move like solid wood will; hence, construction methods are simplified. Sheets of plywood are also fully usable. You can utilize the entire 4 x 8-foot sheet. With solid wood, you need to allow for a minimum of about 20 percent waste. Lastly, plywood comes flat, properly surfaced, and to standard thickness.

The best plywood to use is *birch plywood*. This is readily available in a thickness of ¾, ½, and ¼ inch (in 4 x 8-foot sheets) (**4–1**). Buy one sheet of each, although you can get by with a half sheet (4 x 4 feet) of ¼-inch-thick plywood.

Lumberyards usually carry more high-quality plywood than home centers and will usually cut the larger sheets down to a rough size for you. This makes plywood easier to work with in the shop. When you buy it, specify *veneer-core* (**4–2**), not lumber-or MDF- (medium-density-fiberboard-) core.

There are other hardwood-veneer plywoods available from hardwood suppliers—cherry, oak, walnut, etc. These are also fine, but more expensive. *Lauan* plywood (**4–3**) can be used for cabinets, is available in different thicknesses, and is less expensive than hardwood plywoods.

4–1. *Hardwood plywood shown, from top, in thickness of ¼, ½, and ¾ inch.*

4–2. *Veneer-core plywood. The insides are made of thin, glued-together plies, or veneers.*

4–3. Lauan plywood. It is usable and inexpensive, but is soft and splinters easily.

I've used it, but find it splinters excessively when you saw or drill it. One-quarter-inch lauan plywood is fine, however, for cabinet backs and the bottoms of drawers. Other types of ply-wood—CDX, BC, etc.—are sheathing and deck-ing materials used for building houses.

▼ PREPARING CARCASS COMPONENTS

The first step here is to rip* some plywood to a 12-inch width. I have the lumberyard cut the large 4 × 8-foot sheets in half, to 4 × 4 feet. This allows for a much more *manageable* piece to cut. It's very difficult, and can be dangerous, to try to maneuver an entire 4 × 8-foot sheet of plywood through the saw. I cut two oversized 13 × 48-inch pieces from the 4 × 4-foot piece, and then rip these to the 12-inch width. The point is to make table-saw cuts from something that is a manageable size (**4–5**). This is safer and easier.

The next step is to take the two 12 × 48-inch pieces and crosscut** the final pieces for the car-

*A rip cut is a cut made along the grain of the wood
**A crosscut is a cut made across the grain of the wood.

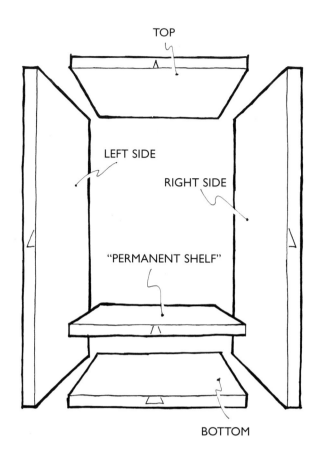

4–4. The five carcass pieces (minus the back), showing pyramid marks for orientation.

cass from them. These are long pieces to crosscut on the table saw, even with the panel cutter. Mark a line across the piece at the 32-inch mark and crosscut this with a jigsaw (**4–6**) or a handheld circular saw. Do this with both the pieces. Now you have manageably sized pieces to crosscut the final pieces from. These final pieces will consist of three 13-inch-wide × 12-inch-deep pieces and two 30-inch-wide × 12-inch-deep pieces.

With the panel cutter in the left miter slot in the table saw, measure over 13 inches from the blade (**4–7**) and make a pencil mark on the fence. Set the stop block, in the closed position, at this mark and clamp it there (**4–8**). Open the stop block (**4–9**). Butt the 32-inch piece to the

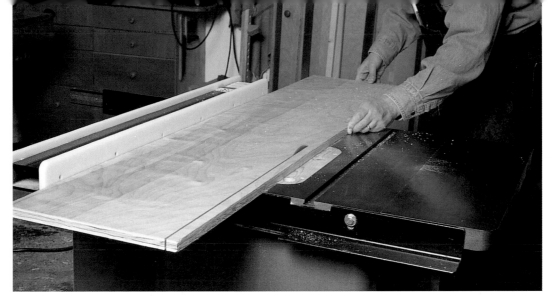

4–5. Making final plywood cuts from a manageably sized piece.

4–6. Using a jigsaw to rough-cut a long piece of plywood.

4–7. Measuring over from the saw blade to the bench stop on the panel cutter.

4–8. Clamping the stop block to the panel-cutter fence.

4–9. Opening the stop block.

4–10. Butting the plywood piece to the open stop block.

4–11. Making the initial crosscut.

4–12. Pulling the panel cutter back after the cut.

block (in the open position) (**4–10**), turn the saw on, and make the crosscut (**4–11**).

Now, pull the panel cutter back, clear of the blade (**4–12**), and turn the saw off. Slide the plywood clear of the stop block; then return the stop block to the closed position. Flip the piece end for end (**4–13**), so that the same edge is against the panel-cutter fence. Turn the saw on and make the second cut (**4–14**). Repeat this with the other 13-inch pieces. When that's done, you can crosscut the two 30-inch pieces the same way (**4–15** and **4–16**).

A few points here: When a larger piece is in the panel cutter, it may want to tip over or to the left, depending on your saw. Keep a hold on the piece at the miter-gauge slot (**4–17**). When you push material forward or back with the jig, hold the workpiece against the fence and down with your left hand, while, at the same time, pushing with your right hand behind the workpiece and holding it down.

Don't try to cut anything smaller than five inches on the panel cutter—it brings your hands too close to the blade. Be aware at all times that the blade is spinning, and keep your hands to the left of the miter-gauge slot. Whenever I use the table saw, I keep my eyes on the spinning blade and repeat to myself, "The saw is on, the saw is on." I make it a point to concentrate fully while the blade spins. This doesn't mean to tense up. Being afraid does no good. Be respectful and concentrate.

4–13. Flipping the piece end for end.

4–14. Making the final cut.

-15. Flipping a 30-inch piece end for end.

4–16. Making a final cut on a 30-inch (side) piece.

4–17. This shows—with no material in the jig—the proper way to hold the panel-cutting jig when making a cut. Both hands press down and feed the jig forward at the position of the miter-gauge slot. The right hand usually pushes the material being cut at the miter-gauge-slot location.

4–18. The carcass pieces marked with pyramids.

4–19. Marking the pieces for biscuit slots using the storypole.

Making the Biscuit Slots and Drilling the Holes

First, mark all the pieces with pyramids (refer to **4–1** and **4–18**), so you know which is the top, bottom, left, and right sides, and shelf piece. With the storypole described in the previous chapter, mark the pieces for the biscuit slots, being sure to hold the stick flush with the front of the pieces (**4–19** and **4–20**). *Note:* After marking the pieces with the pyramids, rip the depth of the shelf piece to 11⅝ inches (final size—13 inches wide × 11⅝ inches deep) (**4–21**). This is to allow for the rabbet in the back.

The biscuit slots are indexed from the bottom of the biscuit-jointer carriage (the base). The distance from the bottom of the carriage to the center of the blade is ⅜ inch (**4–22**). As shown in the previous chapter, all the slot centers on the side pieces will be ⅜ inch from the ends because the machine base and the piece are

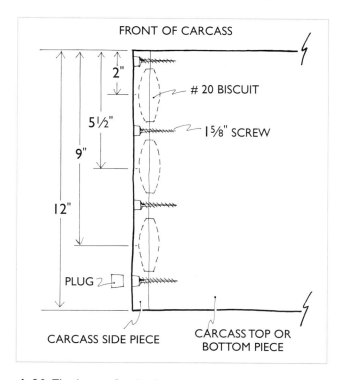

4–20. The layout for the biscuit slots.

4–21. *Ripping the permanent shelf piece to a depth of 11⅝ inches.*

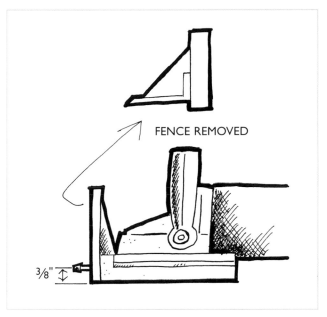

4–22. *The distance from the biscuit-jointer base to the blade center is ⅜ inch.*

indexed on the same plane—the bench stop. Therefore, when the bottom piece is cut, it must have its bottom down. The machine and piece are indexed from the workbench. Thus, when the bottom joins the sides, the slot centers for the bottom and sides are ⅜ inch up from the bottom (**4–23**).

With the top piece, the slot centers have to be

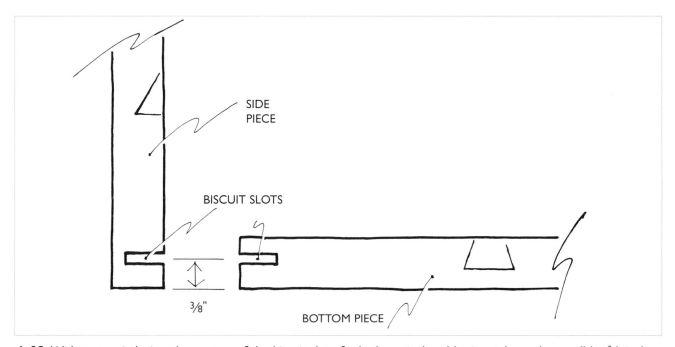

4–23. *With proper indexing, the centers of the biscuit slots, for both vertical and horizontal members, will be ⅜ inch up from the bottom.*

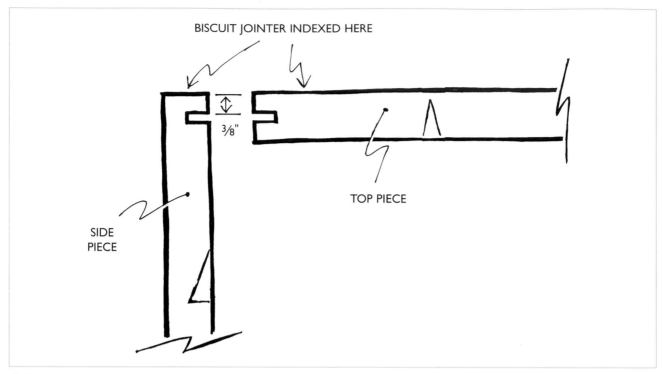

BISCUIT JOINTER INDEXED HERE

⅜"

SIDE
PIECE

TOP PIECE

4–24. *Indexing the top piece slots.*

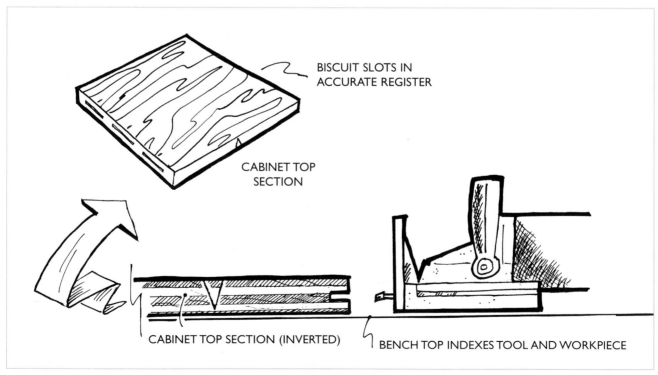

BISCUIT SLOTS IN
ACCURATE REGISTER

CABINET TOP
SECTION

CABINET TOP SECTION (INVERTED)

BENCH TOP INDEXES TOOL AND WORKPIECE

4–25. *For the biscuit slots for the top piece, the piece is turned upside down, so that the slot centers are ⅜ inch from the top.*

⅜ inch *down from the top* (**4–24**), not up from the bottom. When we make the biscuit slots for the top piece, we turn it upside down, so that the slot centers here are ⅜ inch from the top (**4–25**). Then, the top piece also will align flush with the side pieces.

Why, if the plywood is ¾ inch thick, won't the slot be in the middle anyway? Because modern plywoods are 1/32 inch shy of the true ¾-inch thickness. When this carcass is assembled, some of its dimensions will be less than the actual dimensions indicated.

We also need to make a permanent shelf. The shelf piece itself is marked and biscuit-slotted the same way as the bottom piece; that is, it is indexed with the storypole from the front and laid flat on the bench, top up (**4–26**).

The cabinet side pieces must be marked together, for accuracy. Clamp both side pieces together on the workbench, insides up, fronts butted together, and lower edges flush (**4–27**). From the top, measure down 23 inches. Make a mark (**4–28**). Measure down ¾ inch from here and make another mark (**4–29**). Repeat

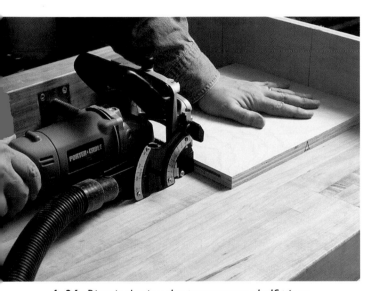

4–26. Biscuit-slotting the permanent shelf piece.

4–27. The two side pieces clamped together.

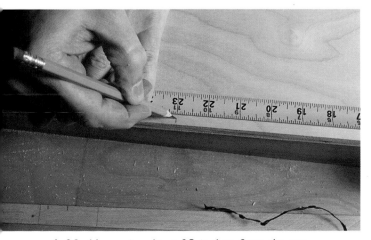

4–28. Measuring down 23 inches from the top.

4–29. Measuring down an additional ¾ inch from the 23-inch mark.

this on the other side. With a straightedge, connect the marks with pencil lines (**4–30**). This gives you the position of the permanent shelf. Mark each side for biscuits using the stick, again indexing from the fronts of the pieces (**4–31**).

Clamp a straightedge across both pieces, flush with the lower pencil line (the line that defines

4–30. Connecting the pencil marks with a straightedge.

4–31. Using the stick to mark for biscuit slots.

4–32. Clamping a straightedge across the two side pieces.

4–33. Resting the biscuit-jointer base on the straightedge.

4–34. *Making the biscuit cuts.*

4–35. *Countersinking the drilled holes.*

the bottom of the shelf) (**4–32**). Rest the base of the biscuit jointer against the straightedge, with the front of the machine resting on the piece (**4–33**). Line up the index mark on the biscuit jointer with the marks on the workpieces and make the biscuit cuts (**4–34**).

With all the biscuit slots cut, you can drill, countersink (**4–35**), make pilot holes in all the pieces, and screw the pieces together (**4–36**) just as in the previous chapter. Be sure to refer to the pyramids to ensure proper alignment of the different parts and to keep the fronts flush.

4–36. *Screwing the carcass pieces together.*

▼ ADJUSTABLE SHELF

Any type of cabinet is best equipped with adjustable shelving. This cabinet has one shelf that is located in the center of the upper area, and which can be adjusted so it's anywhere from 5 to 19 inches from the bottom. It is supported by adjustable shelf pins (**4–37**), inserted into

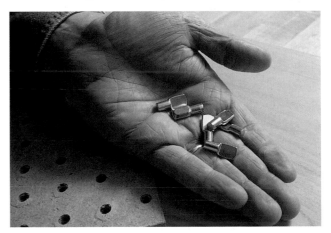

4–37. *Shelf pins.*

4–38. Pegboard is used to make a jig for drilling holes for shelf pins.

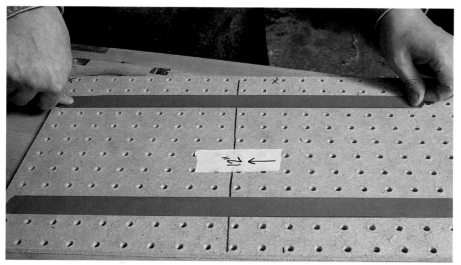

4–39. Applying tape to the pegboard jig.

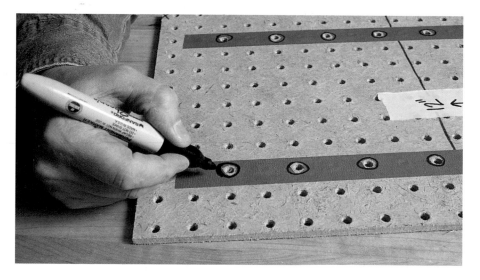

¼-inch holes in either side of the carcass. Before the carcass is assembled, holes must be drilled for the shelf. What is needed are a jig (made of pegboard) and a drill stop (made of scrap wood).

The jig is made from ¼-inch-thick pegboard, with ¼-inch holes one inch from each another (**4–38**). Cut it to a width of 12 inches and a height of 21^{15}/$_{16}$ inches*. With a square, mark a centerline (12 inches long) and then run two strips of tape to either side of the line so that, as shown, by skipping every other hole, you end up with four holes on each side of the centerline (**4–39**). Run the tape on the row of holes about 2½ inches or so from each side. Mark the hole position with a marker (**4–40**). The exact placement of holes from the edges and above and below the centerline isn't critical. What is critical is that the rows of holes are parallel to the edges, so that the shelf sits straight in the cabinet.

Mark the hole positions on both sides of the pegboard. Mark the bottom and one front with X's (**4–41**). The x's are oriented with the bottom of the lower shelf line and the front of each cabinet side piece, so that each series of

The dimensions of the jig aren't critical. What is important is that the two sets of holes are mirror images of each other.

4–40. Marking hole positions with black marker.

holes, when drilled, will mirror each other (**4–42**).

Make a depth stop for the drill bit. Mine is ¾ × ⅞-inch hardwood, with a hole drilled down the center (**4–43**). The length of the bit depends on the length of your ¼-inch drill bit. The bit must stick out ¾ inch from the stop when the bit is chucked in the drill (this allows ¼ inch for the pegboard thickness and ½ inch for the depth of the hole in the carcass side) (**4–44**). I have a screw in mine to hold the depth stop onto the bit, but you don't need to do this. The drill stop will allow you to drill just the right depth each time.

With the drill ready, clamp one of the cabinet

4–41. Marking the bottom and front of the jig with x's.

4–42. The jig in proper position on the side pieces.

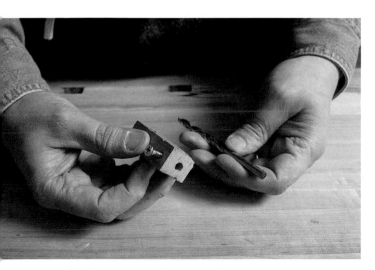

4–43. A depth stop for the drill.

4–44. Setting the correct depth for the drill bit.

4–45. *The jig clamped to the workpiece.*

sides on the workbench—inside facing up—with the jig clamped on top of it (**4–45**). The "✕" edges on the jig are aligned flush with the front of the workpiece and the upper line of the shelf (refer to **4–42**). Holding the drill straight up and down, drill the holes at the positions marked on the tape (**4–46**). Repeat this with the other side piece. You'll need to flip the jig and use the other side, lining up the "✕" sides on the carcass front and shelf line as before.

After assembly, you'll have holes that are properly spaced and mirror each other in position on

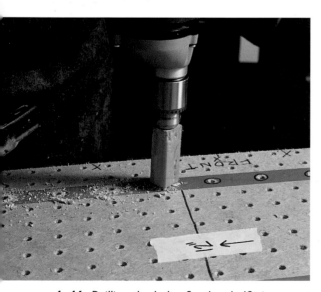

4–46. *Drilling the holes for the shelf pins.*

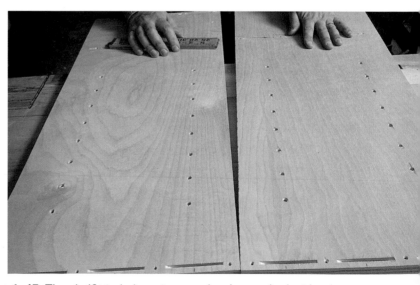

4–47. *The shelf pin holes mirror each other on both side pieces.*

4–48. Crosscutting the adjustable shelf.

each side of the carcass (**4–47**). You can rip and crosscut a shelf now (**4–48**) and try the fit after the carcass is assembled. Make it ⅛ inch shorter in width than the top and bottom and the permanent shelf. It should be about 12⅞ inches wide × 11⅝ inches deep. If you don't like the look of the plies showing, you can cover them with veneer tape (this is covered in Chapter 5).

▼ ASSEMBLY

Putting the carcass together is easy. It's very important to first put together one side and the bottom, shelf, and top, and then the other side. Otherwise, you won't be able to assemble it.

Have the screws ready. Put glue in the biscuit slots for the bottom left and lower corner of the left side piece. Brush glue on three biscuits (**4–49**), put them in the slots, and put the

4–49. Brushing glue on a biscuit.

pieces together, holding them with a squaring block and spring clamps. Drive the screws in. Repeat this with the shelf (in the photographs, the shelf is already assembled) and the top piece. At this point you have an E-shaped assembly (**4–50**). The last step is to glue all the remaining biscuit slots and biscuits, put the other side piece on (**4–51**), and screw it together (**4–52**).

Measure diagonals across the carcass to see if it's square (**4–53**). The measurements should match. If they don't, clamp squaring blocks into opposite corners and measure again. Don't plug the countersink holes yet.

4–50. The E-shaped assembly ready for the final side piece.

4–51. Putting the final side piece on.

4–52. *Screwing the side piece in place.*

4–53. *Measuring the diagonals to see if the carcass is square.*

▼ RABBETING THE BACK

With the ⅜-inch rabbeting bit in the router, you'll need to set it to a ³⁄₁₆-inch cutting depth. If you have a Porter Cable router*, hold the motor and rotate the base until the cutters register flush with the base (**4–54**). Clamp the set-

Although setting the depth of cut varies little from one router to another, it is advisable to refer to your owner's manual for information on this procedure.

4–54. *Setting the cutters of the rabbet bit flush with the router base.*

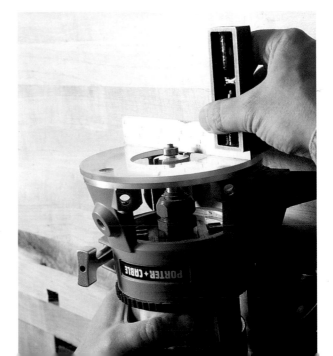

4–55. *The clamping knob on the Porter Cable router.*

ting (**4–55**). After "zeroing" the calibration ring (**4–56**), unclamp the base and turn the motor until the ring shows the depth at ³/₁₆ inch (**4–57**). Clamp this setting again.

After the glue in the carcass has had time to dry—about two hours—you may choose to remove the rearmost screws from each corner*. Clamp the carcass securely, backside up, and rout the rabbet in the carcass back (**4–58** and **4–59**). The D-handle router makes it easier to

**If instructions have been followed, the rearmost screws should not interfere with the router bit as it makes a ³/₈-inch-deep rabbet. If there is any doubt that they may, remove them as is recommended here.*

4–56. *"Zeroing" the calibration ring.*

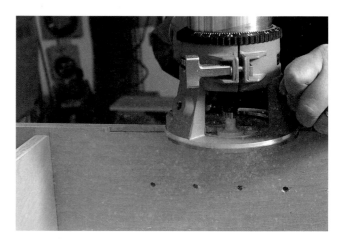

4–58. *Starting the rabbet cut.*

4–57. *Setting the ring depth at ³/₁₆ inch.*

4–59. *The initial ³/₁₆-inch cut.*

4–60. *The D-handled router is easy to balance.*

4–62. *The remaining material being chiseled out.*

4–61. *The material remaining above the permanent shelf.*

4–63. *Resetting depth of cut to ⅜ inch.*

keep the tool level as you do this (**4–60**). Move from right to left, since you are inside the box (outside, it's left to right). Before you begin, hold the router so that the bit is off the work; then start the motor and ease the bit into the inside of the carcass.

The bearing on the rabbeting bit will stop where the shelf is (**4–61**). Stop the router, resume on the other side, and then chisel out this area when you're finished (**4–62**).

When the initial cut is done, reset the router for a ⅜-inch depth of cut (**4–63**) and repeat

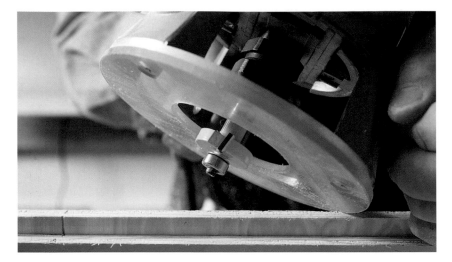

4–64 (left). The ⅜-inch rabbet.

the cut (**4–64**). There is less strain on the router motor, bearings, and the bit, and the chances for splintering the plywood are lessened when the rabbet is cut in two passes. With a chisel, you can square up the corners (**4–65**) and clean out the areas behind the shelf now (**4–66**).

▼ HANGING RAILS

Hanging rails (**4–67**) are two-inch-wide rails that go in the upper and lower back of the cabinet. Because there is a drawer in the bottom of this particular cabinet, I've positioned the lower rail so that it goes above the permanent shelf (which is located on the bottom of the cabinet proper). These rails allow the cabinet to be anchored to a wall by screwing the rails into the wall studs, attaching hanging cleats to them, etc.

Two hanging rails are used per cabinet. They can be made from scrap. They are the same width (13 inches) as the top and bottom pieces of the carcass. You can simply glue them in place. With the carcass face down on

4–65. Chiseling out the corners to square them up.

4–66. Chiseling the area behind the shelf.

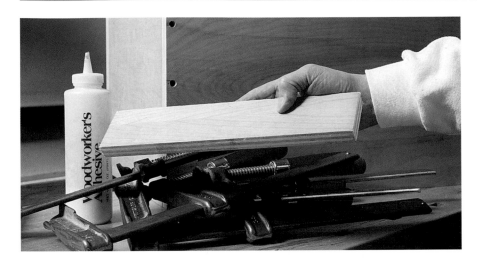

4–67. *A hanging rail.*

the workbench, apply glue to a long edge of the rail (**4–68**) and clamp it in place on the inside of the cabinet *flush with the edge of the rabbet* (**4–69**). Do one rail top and bottom, and let this dry.

4–68. *Applying glue to a hanging rail.*

4–69. *The hanging rails clamped, flush with the rabbet.*

When the hanging rails are in place and the glue set, you can cut the ¼-inch plywood cabinet back. Measure the rabbeted opening. It should be about 14¼ X 29¼ inches. Better yet, take the directly from the opening, marking directly on the ¼-inch plywood (**4–70** and **4–71**).

Rip and crosscut the piece as before. You can nail the back to the carcass with one-inch brads after the drawer guides and kickers are installed (**4–72**). The last step is to plug the countersink holes as before (**4–73** and **4–74**).

Set the carcass aside for now.

4–70. Marking the plywood back width directly from the opening.

4–71. Marking the plywood back height from the opening.

4–72. Nailing the back on with one-inch brads (after drawer assembly and installation).

4–73. Gluing plugs.

4–74. Tapping plugs into the counter-sink holes.

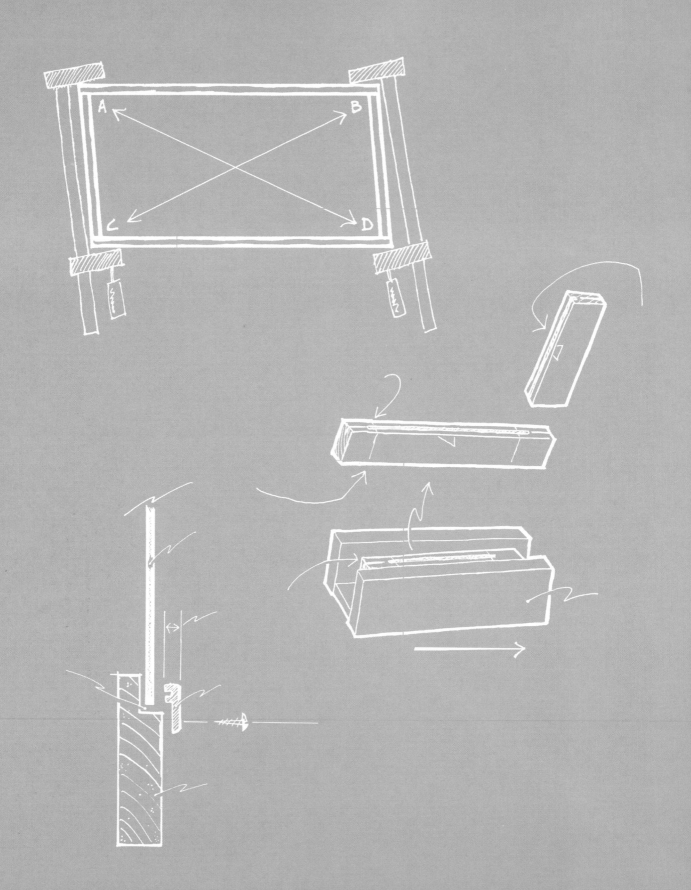

A

B

C

D

CHAPTER

5

Building The Face Frame and Door

▼ MATERIALS

The panel for our cabinet door is made of ¼-inch birch plywood (**5–1**). The face and door frames are made of *solid wood*. Because solid wood is a natural material (unlike plywood, which is a manufactured wood product), it has characteristics that plywood does not. Unlike plywood, it moves (**5–2**). It has knots, checks, and other defects, and can come with "twist" (**5–3**), warped (**5–4**), bowed (**5–5**), cupped (**5–6**)—many different configurations other than flat. This is perfectly normal, since it's a natural (not a man-made) material.

It is beyond the scope of this book to delve into flattening and planing boards. That subject could take up another entire book. Suffice to say, the wood you use needs to be flat and planed to a thickness of ¾ inch. If you don't have a jointer and a planer, some hardwood sup-

5–I. Panel for cabinet.

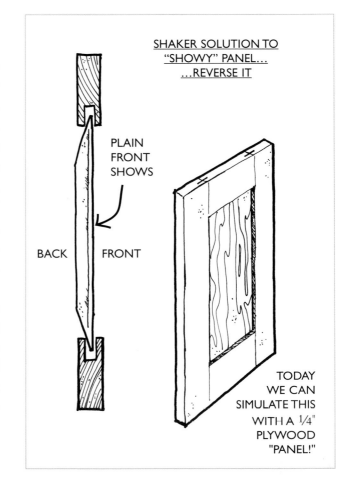

SHAKER SOLUTION TO "SHOWY" PANEL... ...REVERSE IT

PLAIN FRONT SHOWS

BACK   FRONT

TODAY WE CAN SIMULATE THIS WITH A ¼" PLYWOOD "PANEL!"

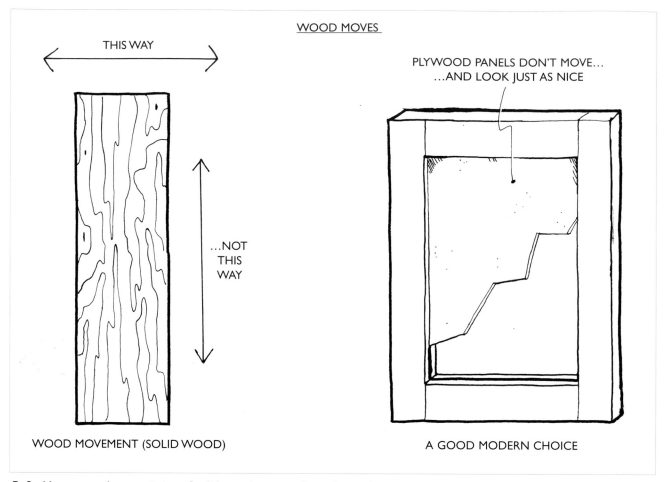

WOOD MOVES

THIS WAY

...NOT THIS WAY

PLYWOOD PANELS DON'T MOVE...
...AND LOOK JUST AS NICE

WOOD MOVEMENT (SOLID WOOD)

A GOOD MODERN CHOICE

5–2. *Movement characteristics of solid wood versus plywood panels.*

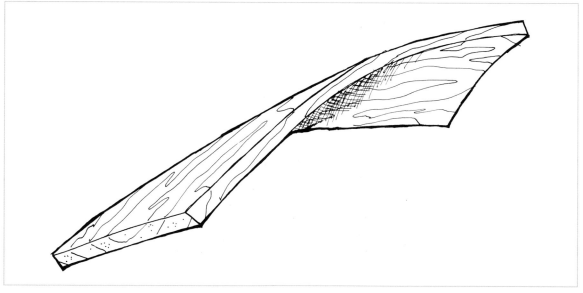

5–3. *Twist.*

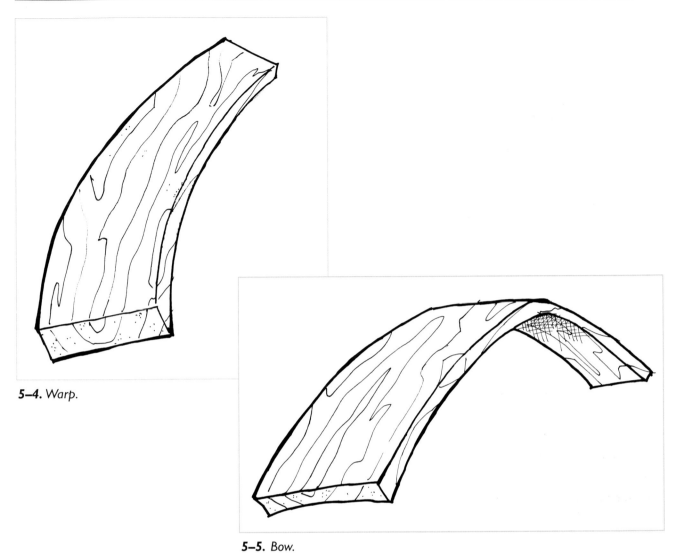

5–4. *Warp.*

5–5. *Bow.*

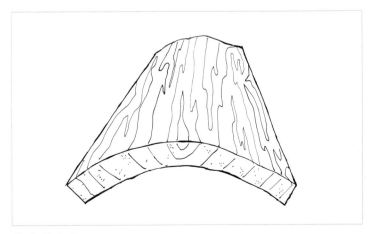

5–6. *Cupping.*

pliers will face-joint and plane the boards for you (face-jointing flattens one face of the board; planing brings the other face parallel and to uniform thickness). Another possibility is to have a local millwork shop dimension the boards for you. You can also flatten and surface the boards by hand, but this is another discipline altogether, beyond the scope of this book.

You may be able to obtain wood that is reasonably flat right off the shelf. If you cannot, you must realize that just running a rough-sawn board through a tabletop planer will not resolve any of its problems, if it has any. Planing a rough-sawn warped board will give you a planed, warped board. Later on, this will create problems, especially when making doors. They will not lie flat against the cabinet.

Which wood to use? Probably the best is *poplar* or *tulipwood*. This is available everywhere, and it's reasonably priced. Many lumberyards stock it, already dimensioned, for finish carpenters. Poplar is a nice, tight-grained hardwood that's easy to work. I don't recommend you use a softwood like pine or spruce.

▼ FACE FRAME

The face frame is an actual frame that is attached to the front of the carcass. The door is hinged to it. It becomes the actual front of the cabinet. It consists of five pieces (refer to **5–12**): top, center, and lower rails and left and right stiles.

As stated previously, the exact dimensions for the face-frame and door parts will not be given because they will vary slightly according to the craftsman's method for working and the tools and materials used. The parts are ¾ inch thick x 2¼ inches wide.

As **5–7** shows, the top of the face frame is flush with the top of the carcass, and the bottom of the face frame extends below the bottom of the carcass. Note that the bottom of the carcass has a ⅛-inch reveal. This is so that the drawer does not ride against the frame member as it's opened. Similarly, the center rail of the face frame is below the shelf ⅛ inch.

Cut the pieces for the frame members. After making the rip cuts, use the panel cutter and stop block for crosscutting (**5–8**), just as with the carcass pieces. I like to plane off the saw

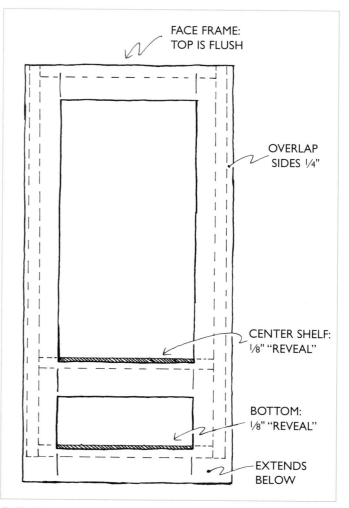

5–7. Here we see the face frame flush with the top of the carcass and extending beyond the bottom of the carcass, as well as the ⅛-inch reveal at the permanent shelf location and the bottom carcass-member location.

5–8. *Crosscutting frame members to size.*

5–9. *Planing off saw marks with a hand plane.*

5–10. *The edge is smooth.*

5–11. *Marking the pieces with pyramids.*

marks with a hand plane (**5–9** and **5–10**) before marking the pieces with pyramids. Keep the plane level as you do this. Mark all the pieces with pyramids (**5–11** and **5–12**), for position.

Clamp the two stiles together on the bench

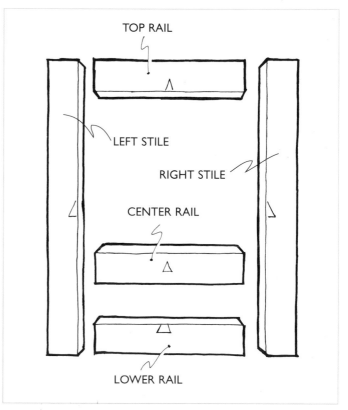

5–12. *The pyramid marking system on a frame assembly.*

5–13. *Clamping the two stiles together for marking.*

with the insides together and the tops flush (**5–13**). Measure and make a line 2¼ inches from the end(s) (**5–14**), just as in Chapter 4. From the top, measure down 23⅛ inches and make a mark (**5–15**). Make a line. Measure down from here 2¼ inches (**5–16**); then mark and make another line (**5–17**).

At this point, all the rail positions are indicated. Now, as in Chapter 3, mark for biscuit slots

5–14. *Making a mark 2¹/4 inches from the ends.*

5–16. *Measuring down 2¹/4 inches.*

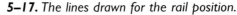

5–17. *The lines drawn for the rail position.*

5–15. *Measuring down from the top 23⅛ inches.*

5–18. *Marking for biscuit slots one inch up from each end.*

5–19. *Measuring up one inch from the bottom to make the mark for center-rail biscuits.*

one inch from each end (**5–18**). For the center rail, measure up one inch from the bottom line and mark for biscuit slots there (**5–19**). Unclamp the stiles, place the rails in position, and transfer the biscuit marks to the rails (**5–20**). At this point, cut all the biscuit slots as the bench.

When all the biscuit slots are cut, set up the two clamping stands on the workbench (refer to pages 37 for information on clamping stands), glue the slots and biscuits, and assemble the frame across the stands. Apply clamps from under the stands (**5–21**). Apply light pressure at first, and make certain the rails line up with the pencil lines on the stiles. Tighten down the clamps and measure the diagonals (**5–22**). If the crosscuts on your table saw were accurate, the diagonals should

5–20. *Transferring the biscuit marks from the stiles to the rails.*

5–21. *Applying clamps with the face-frame assembly on the clamping stands.*

5–22. *Measuring the diagonals to check the face frame for square.*

match. If they don't, refer to **5–23** to see how to "skew" the clamps until they do.

When the glue is dry, saw off the excess biscuits, plane the edges, and sand the face until the members are smooth and even (**5–24**). Saw off the excess biscuit inside the drawer opening (**5–25**); then use a chisel to trim it flush and smooth (**5–26**). With the orbital sander (using 80-grit paper), round over the sharp edges of the face frame, inside and out (**5–27**). You can also

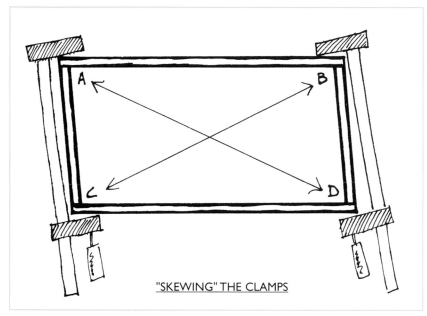

"SKEWING" THE CLAMPS

5–23. *AD is the long diagonal. Skewing the clamps as shown will make the shorter diagonal CB longer. Both should be "equal" (within 1/16 inch).*

5–24. *Sanding the face frame with a orbital sander.*

5–25. *Sawing off the excess biscuit inside the drawer opening.*

5–26. *Trimming the corner flush and smooth with a chisel.*

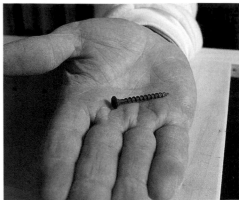

5–28. A 1⅝-inch drywall screw.

5–27 (left). Rounding over the sharp corners with an orbital sander.

use the lower portion of the ⅛-inch round-over bit in the router to do this.

The face frame is screwed to the carcass with 1⅝-inch screws (**5–28**). If the carcass members aren't dead flush at the front, you can belt-sand them flush (an 80-grit belt is fine) (**5–29**). Clamp the face frame to the carcass (**5–30**), making sure that its top is flush with the carcass (**5–31**); the sides should extend ¼ inch out from the carcass on each side (**5–32**), the lower rail

5–29. Belt-sanding the carcass members flush.

5–31. *The top of the face frame is flush with the carcass top.*

5–30. *The face frame is clamped to the carcass.*

5–32. *The face-frame sides should extend 1/4 inch out from the carcass on each side.*

should extend below the bottom carcass member ⅛ inch (**5–33**), and the center rail should extend below the permanent shelf ⅛ inch (**5–34**). I drill and countersink for screws about every four inches around the rails and stiles (**5–35** and **5–36**). The countersink holes are plugged (**5–37**) and trimmed (**5–38** and **5–39**).

5–33. The lower rail extends below the face frame ⅛ inch.

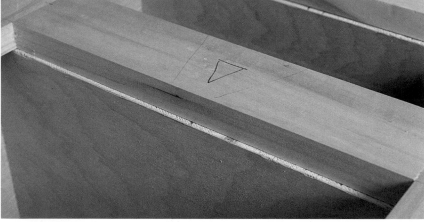

5–34. The center rail extends below the permanent shelf ⅛ inch.

5–35. Drilling and countersinking for screws.

5–36. Drilling a screw in place.

5–37. Tapping in a plug.

5–38. Trimming the plug with a chisel.

5–39. Sanding plugs flush with the face frame.

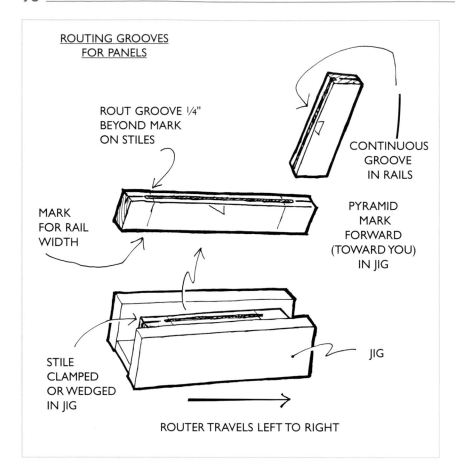

ROUTING GROOVES
FOR PANELS

ROUT GROOVE ¼"
BEYOND MARK
ON STILES

CONTINUOUS
GROOVE
IN RAILS

MARK
FOR RAIL
WIDTH

PYRAMID
MARK
FORWARD
(TOWARD YOU)
IN JIG

STILE
CLAMPED
OR WEDGED
IN JIG

JIG

ROUTER TRAVELS LEFT TO RIGHT

▼ FRAME-AND-PANEL DOOR

The door is built using the same construction principles as the face frame, except that there is a groove routed in the inside edges to accept the ¼-inch plywood panel (**5–40**). It overlaps the face frame door by ⅜ inch at the top, sides, and bottom. The door's rails and stiles are prepared and biscuit-slotted the same way as the face frame's, with the following exception: Instead of measuring up one inch from each stile end, we measure up ½ inch. This allows enough clearance for the routed groove, which holds the panel (**5–41**).

5–40. *Routing grooves for panels.*

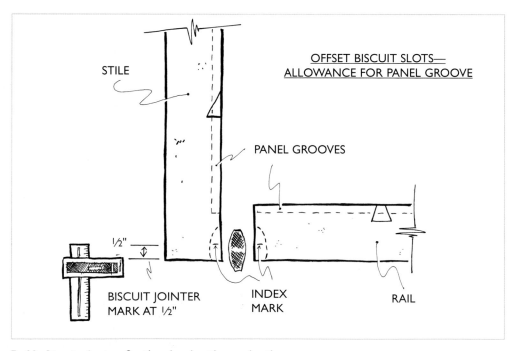

STILE

OFFSET BISCUIT SLOTS—
ALLOWANCE FOR PANEL GROOVE

PANEL GROOVES

½"

BISCUIT JOINTER
MARK AT ½"

INDEX
MARK

RAIL

5–41. *Biscuit-slotting for the door's stiles and rails.*

The groove is routed in the mortise or router jig (refer to pages 41 and 42) with a plunge router and a ¼-inch router bit (**5–42**). Either a spiral or a straight-cutting bit will work (**5–43**). The groove is *stopped* on the stiles, to allow for the biscuit slot; on the rails, the groove is *continuous* (**5–44**).

5–43. *Straight-fluted router bit (top), and spiral upcut bit (bottom).*

5–42. *A vacuum-equipped 2½-horsepower router in position on the router jig.*

5–44. *Stopped groove in stile (top), and continuous groove in rail (bottom).*

Clamp the mortise jig to the workbench (**5–45**). The router rides on top of the U-shaped channels, with the edge-guide bearing against the outside of the channel closest to you (**5–46**). On a piece of scrap the same thickness and width as the rails and stiles, use a combination square to draw a line down the center of one long-grain edge (**5–47**). Clamp this piece in the jig with the centerline up, with the top of the workpiece flush with the top of the jig's channel (**5–48**).

5–46. Router and edge guide in position on the router jig.

5–45. The mortise jig clamped to the workbench.

5–47. Drawing a line down the center of a scrap piece.

5–48. Clamping the scrap piece in the jig. Because this jig is quite long, the right end of the workpiece is held in place with wedges.

edge guide until this is obtained. The cut doesn't need to be exactly dead center; since all the pieces will be oriented the same way in the jig, all the grooves will line up on all the pieces.

When the plunge-router setup is correct, take a stile and extend the end line (not the biscuit mark) onto the inside edge (**5–51**). Make a mark ¼ inch toward the end of the stile (**5–52**) and extend the line across the edge (**5–53**). This shows you where to stop the cut for the groove.

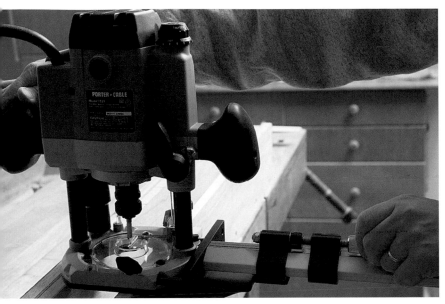

5–49. Adjusting the edge guide.

The next step in the grooving operation is to set up the router. The ¼-inch bit is set for a ⁵⁄₁₆-inch cut in two passes. Put the edge guide on the router and, with the router on top of the jig, adjust the edge guide (**5–49**); the bit must make a cut that cuts through the center of the line (**5–50**). In other words, the bit must make a ¼-inch groove in *about* the center of the piece. Keep adjusting, readjusting, and tightening the

5–51. Extending the line on the stile face to the edge.

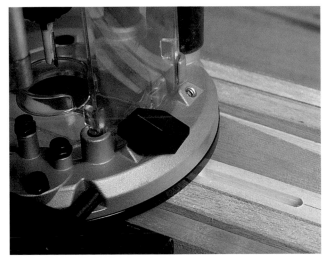

5–50. The ¼-inch bit will bisect the line, indicating that the edge guide is correctly positioned.

5–52. Making the ¼-inch mark.

5–53. Extending a line from the ¼-inch mark across the edge of the stile. This indicates the extent of the groove in the stile.

When the workpieces are clamped in the jig, be sure that the pyramid marks are facing you, that is, *to the inside* (**5–54**). This ensures that the groove will be in the same position on all the pieces. Put the rails in the jig and rout them first. The groove on the rails runs continuously across the piece. Next, do the stiles. Start the plunge cut at the ¼-inch mark you made on one end, and finish on the same mark on the other end (**5–55** and **5–56**).

You now should have two rails and two

stiles with properly routed ¼-inch grooves to accept the plywood panel. Rip (**5–57**) and cross-cut the ¼-inch plywood to make a panel to the correct size to fit into the door frame. It should be about 7⅜ x 17⅜ inches.

Dry-fit the rails, stiles, and panel until you are satisfied that the panel fits inside. If anything, the panels should have a *slight* amount of movement inside the frame to allow for the solid wood shrinking and swelling. This isn't critical—for this size door, the wood movement is very slight. When the fit is good, glue up the slots (**5–58**) and the biscuits, and, as was done with the face frame, clamp the assembly over the clamping stands. Check the diagonals for square (**5–59**) and readjust the clamps if necessary.

5–55. A groove routed in the stile. Note the wedges.

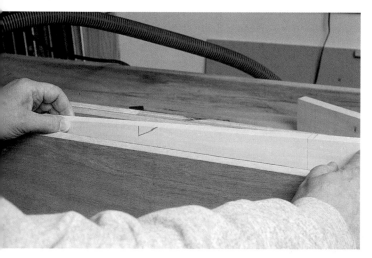

5–54. Placing a stile in the mortise (router) jig with the pyramid mark facing the operator.

5–56. The groove properly stopped at the 1/4-inch mark.

5–57 (above). Ripping the 1/4-inch plywood panel.

5–58. Applying glue to the biscuit slots.

5–59. Measuring the diagonals to see if the door is square.

5–60. Sawing the excess biscuit with a gent's saw.

5–61. The door edges being planed smooth.

Hanging the Door

When the glue is dry, saw off the excess biscuits (**5–60**), plane the edges smooth (**5–61**), and sand the door parts flush (**5–62**). Round over the edges slightly (**5–63**), as you did with the face frame. With the door sanded, lay it facedown on the workbench. I am assuming we want the door to swing left when opened, so we will mount the hinges on the right side here, since the door is lying facedown.

We are using a ⅜-inch overlap hinge (**5–64**). These are easy to install, are self-closing, adjustable, and look okay. The door overlaps ⅜-inch into the hinge itself, which is why we have made our door ⅜ inch bigger in each dimension than the door opening in the cabinet (**5–65**). It's also a very forgiving hinge design—good for beginners or professionals!

5–62. Sanding the door parts flush.

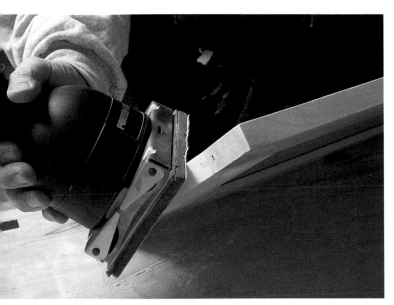

5–63. *Rounding over the sharp edges of the door with an orbital sander.*

5–64. *A ⅜-inch overlap hinge.*

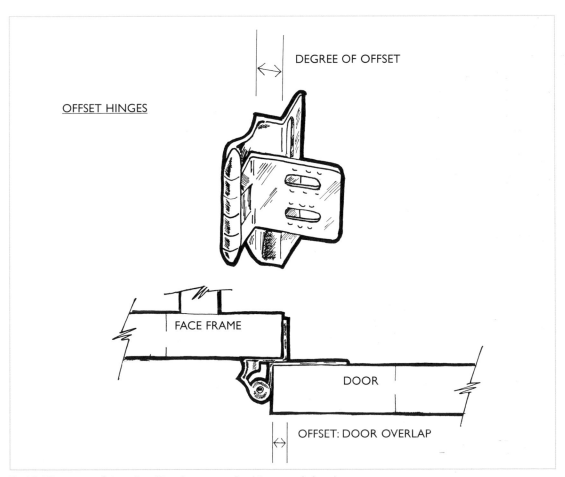

DEGREE OF OFFSET

OFFSET HINGES

FACE FRAME

DOOR

OFFSET: DOOR OVERLAP

5–65. *There is a ⅜-inch offset between the hinge and the door.*

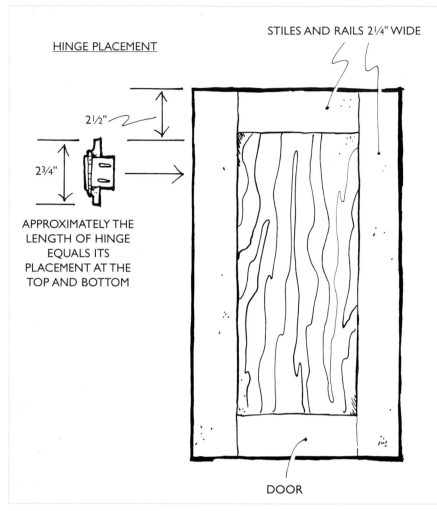

HINGE PLACEMENT

STILES AND RAILS 2¼" WIDE

2½"

2¾"

APPROXIMATELY THE
LENGTH OF HINGE
EQUALS ITS
PLACEMENT AT THE
TOP AND BOTTOM

DOOR

5–66. Hinge placement on the cabinet door.

The hinge is placed about 2½ inches from the top and bottom of the door (**5–66**). Measure up from the bottom of the door 2½ inches. This is where the knuckle of the hinge should be (**5–67**). With the hinge in the open position, screw the hinge to the door by driving screws through the flat flange into the door (**5–68**). Drill pilot holes for the screws, being careful not to drill through the other side (**5–69**). Repeat this for installing the top hinge, this time measuring *down* 2½ inches for the knuckle position (**5–70**).

With the cabinet on the workbench, clamp a piece of scrap to it ⅜ inch below the door opening (**5–71**). The combination square makes it simple to get it right (**5–72**).

5–67. Measuring up 2½ inches from the door bottom to the hinge knuckle.

5–68. Screwing the hinge to the door.

5–69. *Pilot-hole drilling.*

5–71. *A piece of scrap clamped 3/8 inch below the door opening.*

5–70. *Measuring down 2½ inches for the top hinge position.*

5–72. *Using a combination square to set the 3/8-inch distance from the door opening to the piece of scrap.*

With the hinges still in the open position, rest the door on the scrap piece and line up the upper flange on the inside stile of the face frame (**5–73**). Mark the screw position in the center of the slot in the hinge flange with an awl (**5–74**) and remove the door. Drill a pilot hole for the screw, put the door in position again, and drive the screw in (**5–75**). Once this is done, drill a pilot hole and drive a screw into the lower flange as well. Remove the scrap piece and close the door. It should look even and very fine when closed (**5–76**).

At this point, take the door off the cabinet and put the knob on. At the width and length center point of the stile opposite the hinges, make a mark with an awl (**5–77**). In this example, I'm

5–74. *Marking a screw position with an awl.*

5–73. *Resting the door on the scrap piece to line up the hinge on the face frame.*

5–75. *Screwing the hinge to the face frame. The small size of this drill/driver is a great advantage here.*

5–76. The door in place on the cabinet with an even reveal.

5–77. Marking with an awl for knob position on the door.

5–78. Applying glue to a cabinet knob tenon.

5–79. Tapping the cabinet knob in place with a rubber mallet.

using a Shaker-style knob with a ⅜-inch tenon. You may choose to drill a smaller hole for a knob that's held in place with a screw. If you use a knob with a tenon, drill the hole, apply glue to the hole and the tenon (**5–78**), and tap the knob in with a mallet (**5–79**).

When you have the knob on, you can reinstall

5–80. The completed and hung door.

5–81. Ripping plywood for the solid door. Most of the feed pressure is with my right hand, keeping the piece against the fence and avoiding kickback.

the door with the remaining screws (**5–80**). The cabinet is almost completed now except for the drawer.

▼ DOOR OPTIONS

There are other door designs you can make, depending on the type of look desired or the function of the cabinet. They are discussed below.

Solid Doors

Solid doors are very easy to make and give a more modern appearance. You can make them out of solid-wood panels, but it's easier to use plywood. For the cabinet we are making in this section, you can use birch plywood. Cut the door to the correct dimensions* (**5–81**), being

*Because we are using ⅜-inch overlap hinges, the door should be sized to overlap the opening ⅜ inch in all directions.

5–82. *Scoring the plywood with a knife along the cut line to avoid tear-out.*

5–83. *The cut line.*

5–84. *Wood-veneer edging tape has heat-activated glue on its back.*

5–85. *Tools for using wood-veneer tape: tape, clothes iron, hammer, file, and sandpaper.*

sure to avoid tear-out, especially on the front side that shows. An easy way is to mark the cut line with a knife when you crosscut the piece (**5–82** and **5–83**).

Once the door is cut, you can add edging to it to hide the plies. An easy way to do this is to use wood-veneer tape, with heat-activated glue on the back (**5–84** and **5–85**). Clamp the door in the bench vise and cut off a strip of tape about one inch longer than the edge you're working on (**5–86**). The tape is wider than ¾ inch, so center

5–86. *Cutting the tape to length.*

it as you pass an iron over it, working down the plywood edge (**5–87**). Set the iron on the "cotton" setting. Pass the iron back and forth over the veneer tape slowly about four or five times. Be sure not to burn the tape. Put the iron down and immediately burnish the tape again with a steel hammerhead (**5–88**). The mass of steel in the hammer absorbs heat and secures the tape.

With a wood file, you now trim the veneer tape. Hold the file angled slightly outward from the side and run it down and sideways along the length of the tape (**5–89**). It will take a few passes to cut through the tape. There is no need to push too hard—use moderate pressure. After a little practice, you'll get the hang of it. Repeat this on the other side and at the ends. When you're through with filing, use 120-grit sandpaper to smooth over the corners (**5–90**). Repeat this on the other three edges of the door.

5–87. Using the iron to adhere the tape to the piece, while keeping the tape centered on the edge with my other hand.

5–89. A wood file trims off the excess veneer tape.

5–88. The heavy steel hammerhead absorbs the heat and burnishes the tape down for a strong bond.

5–90. Sandpapering the edges lightly produces a flaw-less-looking edge.

5–91. *The solid door installed on the cabinet.*

After the door is edged, it can be installed just as the frame-and-panel door was (**5–91**).

Glass-and-Mirror Doors

A frame-and-panel door with glass instead of the ¼-inch panel is useful for display cabinets. You can also use a mirror instead of a panel for making a medicine cabinet for a bathroom. Lots of kitchen cabinet and hutch designs utilize glass panel doors for showing off dinnerware, wine glasses, etc. It's useful to know how to make them.

To make a door like this, the door frame is assembled the same way as with the frame-and-panel door; there is no need to rout the groove in the members, however. When the glue is dry after assembly, the back of the door is routed out with a ⅜-inch rabbeting bit in the router (**5–92**). This is done much the same way as with the cabinet back; the depth of the rabbet depends on the thickness of the glass and the thickness of the retaining clips (**5–93**).

5–92. *The rabbet at the back of the door routed out and the corners squared with a chisel.*

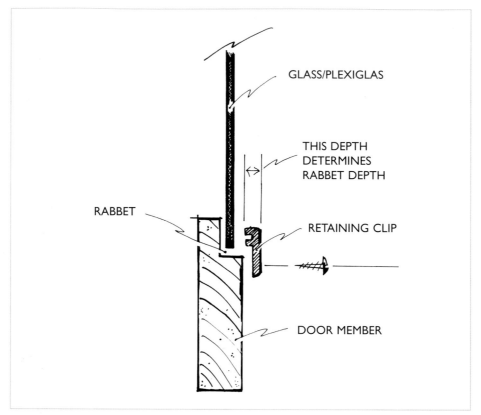

GLASS/PLEXIGLAS

THIS DEPTH
DETERMINES
RABBET DEPTH

RABBET

RETAINING CLIP

DOOR MEMBER

5–93. The thickness of the glass/Plexiglas and the type of retaining clip you use determines the depth of the rabbet cut in the door.

5–94. Retaining clips hold the panel member in place and allow easy removal if need be.

It's best to have the retaining clips and a sample of the glass thickness on hand before making the rabbet. The clips I use allow a ¼-inch rabbet for single-thickness glass (**5–94**). Be sure to test before making the rabbet. The clips allow the glass or mirror to be replaced in case of damage (I would recommend using tempered glass).

This type of door design can accommodate all types of door-panel material—different plywoods, decorative Plexiglas (**5–95**), or even fabric-covered or painted panels (**5–96**). The possibilities are endless.

5–95. *Decorative Plexiglas installed as the "panel."*

5–96. *Fabric covering a thin board used as the door panel.*

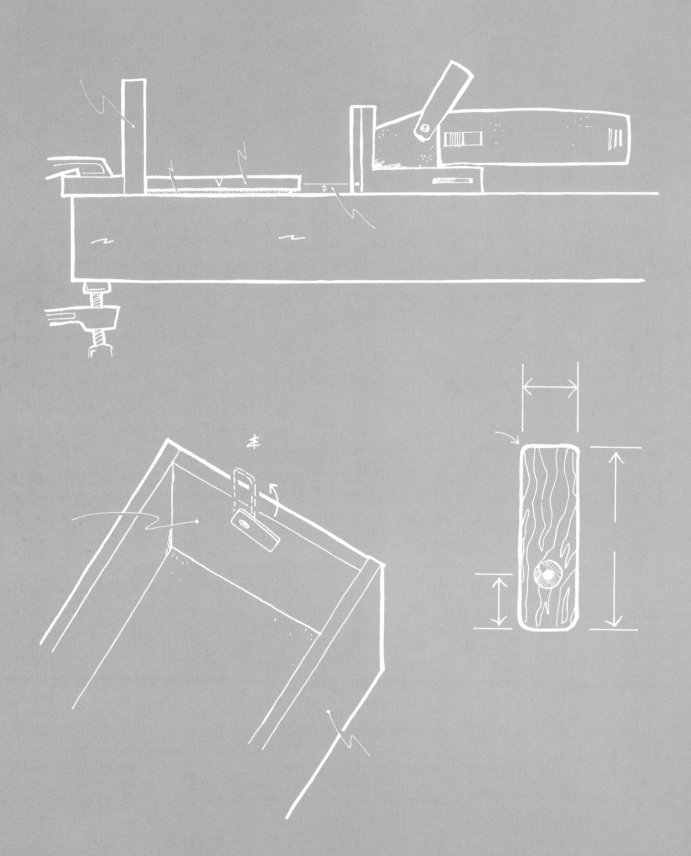

CHAPTER

6

Making the Drawer

The drawer for our cabinet (**6–1**) has an applied front. The drawer box is 11 inches deep by the width and height of the drawer opening: about 3⅞ x 10½ inches. The bottom of the drawer is ¼-inch-thick plywood, lauan, or birch. It rides in a groove in the front and sides of the drawer, and is nailed to the back. There are side guides, backstops, and "kickers" installed in the cabinet so the drawer will operate smoothly (**6–2**).

▼ MATERIALS

The drawer is made from ½-inch-thick birch plywood and is biscuited together with #10 biscuits.

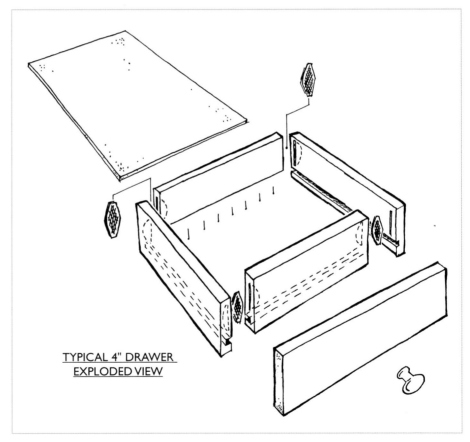

TYPICAL 4" DRAWER
EXPLODED VIEW

6–1. An exploded view of the cabinet drawer. It is 11 inches deep and approximately 3⅞ inches wide and 10½ inches high. It has an applied front and a ¼-inch-thick plywood bottom that rides in a groove in the front and sides of the drawer and is nailed to the back.

The reason we use #10 biscuits is because the material is thinner (**6–3**); the biscuit-jointer blade, set at the #20 setting, would cut through the outside of the drawer-box side (**6–4**). The applied front is whatever hardwood you make the other solid-wood parts from—in this case, poplar.

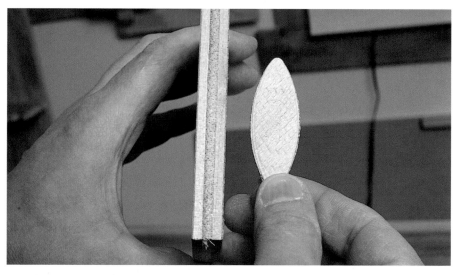

6–2. *A smoothly operating drawer.*

6–3. *The narrow #10 biscuit is good for ¹/₂-inch-thick plywood.*

6–4. *A deeper #20 biscuit slot will penetrate ¹/₂-inch-thick plywood.*

▼ DRAWER PARTS

The first step is to measure the drawer opening, from top to bottom. The face-frame opening is 4 inches, minus the ⅛-inch reveal of the carcass bottom. Therefore, the opening should be about 3⅞ inches (the drawer box can be belt-sanded to final fit later) (**6–5**). From the ½-inch plywood, rip about 40 inches of this material at this width (**6–6**).

6–5. Measuring the drawer opening, from top to bottom (height of the drawer).

6–6. Ripping a length of ½-inch plywood.

At the table saw, set the stop block on the panel cutter for an 11-inch crosscut (this is the length of the drawer sides) (**6–7**). Cut the drawer-box sides to this measurement (**6–8** and **6–9**).

Now measure the drawer-opening *width* in the face frame. It should be about 10½ inches (**6–10**). Subtract from this dimension the width of both drawer sides and an additional ⅛ inch.

6–7. Setting the stop block to 11 inches (the length of the drawer sides).

6–8. Crosscutting the drawer sides; note that the stop block is "open."

6–9. Crosscutting the drawer sides; the stop block is "closed."

6–10. Measuring the drawer-opening width.

6–11. Marking the drawer components with pyramids.

This dimension should be about 9⁷⁄₁₆ inches. Set this dimension to the stop block on the panel cutter and crosscut two pieces—these are the front and the back. Mark all the pieces with pyramids (**6–11**).

Next, a groove is cut in the lower inside of the front and side pieces for the drawer bottom to ride in. The back is also ripped again to a width equaling the distance from the top of the drawer to the top of the groove. This is done so the drawer bottom can be nailed to the bottom of the back piece.

6–12. A "wobble" dado-head cutter. The hub in the middle of the unit is adjusted to control the degree of "wobble" (eccentric spin), and thus the width of the cut.

The groove starts about ¼ inch up from the bottom and is about ¼ inch deep. The easiest way to cut it is with a dado head on the table saw. Either a "wobble" dado head (**6–12**) or a "stack" dado head (**6–13**) can be used. The wobble dado head is fast to set up, but doesn't leave an absolutely flat bottom. The stack dado head is more time-consuming to set up, but cuts a bit more precisely (**6–14**). Test the cutting on a piece of scrap until the groove is the correct size and in position; then cut a groove in the front and side drawer pieces (**6–15** and **6–16**).

When the grooves are cut in the front and

6–13. A "stack" dado-head cutter. Cutters of various widths are "stacked" within the two outside plates to control the width of cut.

6–14. A ¼-inch groove cut with a wobble dado head (top) and the stack dado head (bottom). For a groove this narrow, either dado head is acceptable (usually the stack dado head produces a crisper, more well-defined cut, but for something this narrow, either dado head is fine).

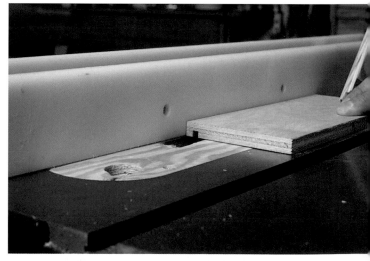

6–15. Using a dado head to cut the ¼-inch groove for the drawer bottom.

6–16. The groove cut.

6–17 (right)**.** Ripping the drawer back to correct width. Note the push stick.

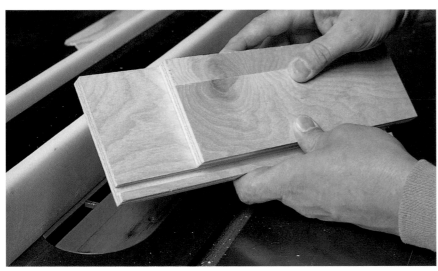

6–18. The width of the drawer back is equal to the distance from the top of the groove to the top of the drawer piece. Here a drawer back is held in front of a side piece.

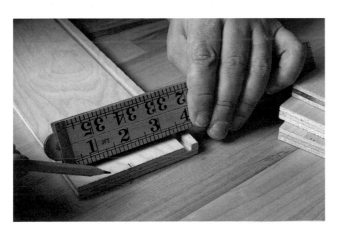

sides, replace the dado head with the blade and rip the drawer back to size (**6–17**). In **6–18**, you can see the correct relationship between the drawer back and one of the other three pieces.

Now mark the pieces for biscuit-slotting. This mark should be made in the middle of the drawer width *above the groove* (on the drawer described here, it would be about $1^{11}/_{16}$ inch

6–19. Marking the drawer pieces for biscuit slots.

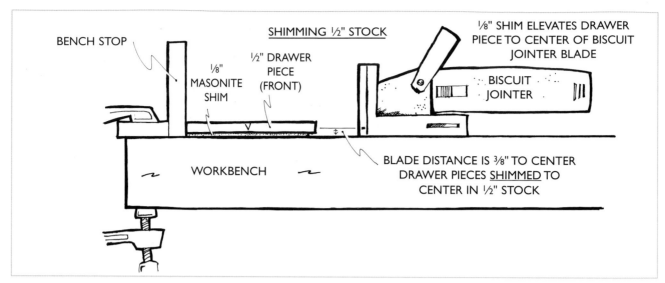

6–20. *Technique for shimming a ½-inch-thick drawer front.*

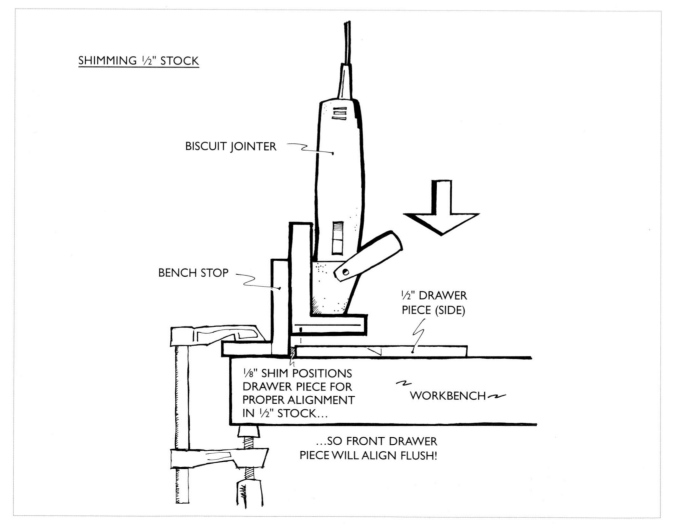

6–21. *Technique for shimming a ½-inch-thick drawer side.*

6–22. One-eighth-inch Masonite pieces are used for shims when biscuit-slotting ½-inch-thick plywood.

6–23. For the front and back pieces, the shim goes between the workbench and the workpiece.

6–24. Biscuit-slotting a front piece. The shim is visible below the piece.

above the groove); this is also the center of the back piece. Mark for biscuit slots, remembering that the front and back are slotted into the ends, and the sides slotted into their face ends (as with their carcass sides) (**6–19**).

Because the plywood is ½ inch thick, and the distance from the biscuit-jointer base to the blade center is ⅜ inch, the drawer pieces need to be shimmed ⅛ inch for the biscuit-slotting (**6–20** and **6–21**). One-eighth-inch Masonite is a good choice for shim material (**6–22**). For the front and back pieces, the shim goes between the piece and the workbench (**6–23** to **6–25**). For the side pieces, the shim goes between

6–25. The biscuit slot cut in the front piece.

6–26. Placing the shim between the side piece and the bench stop. The shim is ⁷/₁₆ inch wide—it must be slightly thinner than the plywood width.

6–27. Lining up the biscuit mark on a side piece with the line on the bench stop.

the bench stop and the work-piece (**6–26** to **6–29**).

When the pieces are grooved and biscuit-slotted, assemble the drawer box (**6–30**). Use two clamps to hold the assembly together (**6–31**). Make sure the drawer-box parts are flush at the top.

With the drawer box glued and clamped, measure for the drawer bottom. The width is the side-to-side dimension within the grooves. The length is the dimension from the end of the groove in the box front to the back of the drawer. Rip and crosscut a piece of ¼-inch plywood to these dimensions. This is the drawer bottom.

6–28. Cutting the biscuit slot in the side piece.

6–29. The biscuit slot cut in the side piece.

6–30. Gluing up the drawer pieces for assembly.

6–31. The drawer box held in place with clamps.

6–32. A bit of glue goes in the front groove before the drawer bottom is inserted.

I put a drop of glue in the front groove before inserting the drawer bottom (**6–32**). Make sure it's square before nailing it to the bottom of the back piece (**6–33**).

6–33. Checking the drawer box for square before the bottom is nailed to the back.

Kickers and Side Guides

When the drawer box is dry, check to see if it slides into the opening without scraping the upper face-frame rail (**6–34**). If the fit here is tight, clamp the drawer box in the bench and belt-sand the top until there is clearance (**6–35**). With an orbital sander, round over all the drawer-box edges, top and bottom (**6–36**).

Guides have to be installed in the sides of the cabinet, so the drawer will pull out straight. The width of the side guides will be about 1⁵/₁₆ inch. I use scrap from the face-frame and door parts. The guides should extend ¹/₁₆ inch into the opening (so the drawer rides on the side guides, not the stiles) (**6–37** and **6–38**). Try the guides with the drawer in place and trim them as

6–34. Testing the drawer box for fit in the cabinet.

6–35. Belt-sanding the drawer-box edges.

6–36. Rounding over the sharp edges of the drawer box with the orbital sander.

6–37. *A side guide in place in the lower-right drawer opening.*

necessary. The dimensions given are somewhat approximate. As in any woodworking, just following the measurements doesn't guarantee success. You must try the fit to get it just right. When the fit is good, screw the side guides into the cabinet from the bottom. I clamp them in place and screw them in from underneath (**6–39**).

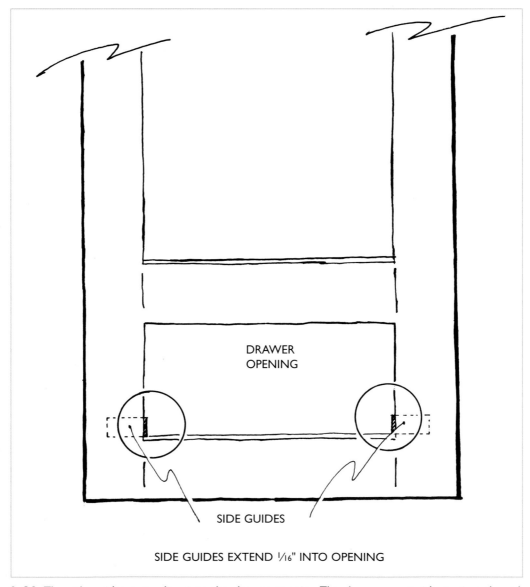

DRAWER
OPENING

SIDE GUIDES

SIDE GUIDES EXTEND ¹⁄₁₆" INTO OPENING

6–38. *The side guides extending into the drawer opening. The drawer must ride against the side guide, not the face fame.*

The "kickers" are installed above the drawer to prevent it from dropping down as it's opened. You can place one kicker in the center of the opening, but I like to use two kickers above each drawer side (**6–40**). Kickers should extend about ¹⁄₁₆ inch above the face frame, so in my cabinet this measurement is 1⁹⁄₁₆ inch. Again, check the fit in your own cabinet to be certain. Clamp the kickers in position and screw them in place from above (**6–41**). The kickers and the back-stop installation are the reasons we wait to add a plywood back to the cabinet.

6–39. With the side guides clamped in place, they are screwed in place from the bottom of the cabinet.

6–40. "Kickers" in place in the drawer opening.

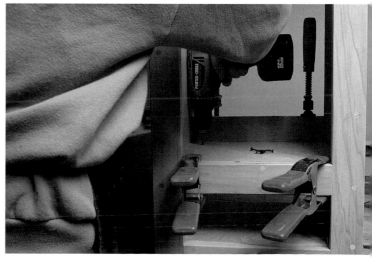

6–41. Screwing the kickers in place. Note that clamps hold the kickers in place front and back.

6–42. Rounding over the edges of the drawer front with the orbital sander.

6–43. Drilling and countersinking the pilot holes inside the drawer box.

Drawer Front

The drawer front, like the door, is ⅜ inch larger in every dimension than the opening, so it is about 4¾ x 11⅜ inches. Round over all the edges and corners slightly (**6–42**). In the drawer box, drill and countersink six pilot holes as shown in **6–43**. On the workbench, position the drawer front in position under the drawer box so the overlap is even in all directions (**6–44**). With a one-inch screw, fasten the box to the front through the top center hole (**6–45**). Put the drawer in the opening and check the front (**6–46**). Adjust the front, if necessary, until it looks straight and even; then carefully remove and fasten it with additional screws (**6–47**). At this point, you can install a knob as you did with the cabinet door.

Backstops and Drawer Stop

Rip the ⅜-inch-thick stock for the back and drawer stops from larger pieces; then crosscut them to the smaller sizes.*

Specific dimensions are not given because the room available for the stop will vary from cabinetmaker to cabinetmaker. The stops should be small enough to fit into the drawer, but not so small that securing them with a screw will split them.

6–44. Obtaining an even overlap for the drawer front.

6–45. *Attaching the drawer front with a screw through the top center hole.*

6–46 (left). *Checking that the drawer front is straight and even.*

6–47. *Fastening the drawer front with additional screws.*

With the drawer in the cabinet opening, place two business cards behind the drawer-front overlap on each side of the drawer (**6–48**). Lightly clamp the drawer in this position (**6–49**). At the back of the drawer opening, butt the backstops in position behind the drawer sides and against the side guide and screw them in place (**6–50**). Remove the clamps. I use poplar scrap to make the backstops. The object is to have the drawer hit the stops before the drawer front hits the face frame. The drawer front sits proud of the face frame by the thickness of the business cards.

The drawer stop (**6–51** and **6–52**) prevents the drawer from being yanked completely out of the opening. Screw it in place in the center of

6–48. Placing two business cards between the drawer-front overlap and the face frame.

6–49. Lightly clamping the drawer front in place.

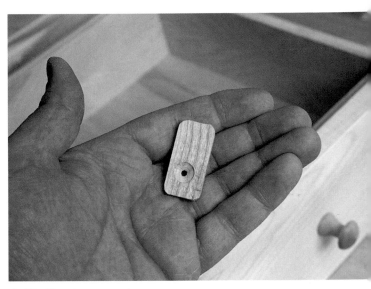

6–50. *A backstop screwed in place behind the drawer box.*

6–51. *The drawer stop.*

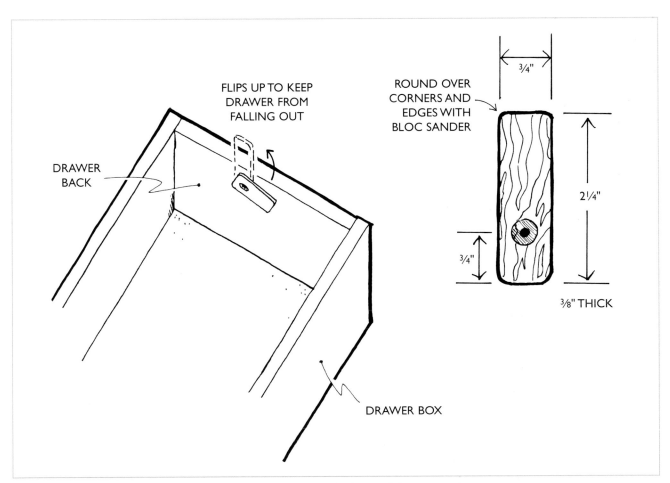

FLIPS UP TO KEEP DRAWER FROM FALLING OUT

ROUND OVER CORNERS AND EDGES WITH BLOC SANDER

3/4"

2 1/4"

3/4"

3/8" THICK

DRAWER BACK

DRAWER BOX

6–52. *The drawer stop prevents the drawer from being yanked out of the opening.*

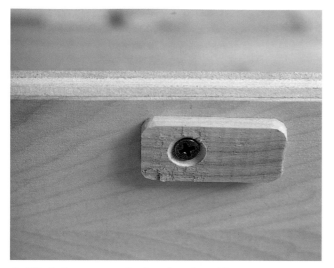

6–53. *A drawer stop in the closed position.*

6–54. *A drawer stop in the open position.*

the back so it clears the top of the drawer when in the down position (**6–53** and **6–54**). Push the drawer into the opening slightly (**6–55**), reach your hand in, and turn the drawer stop upward (**6–56**).

All the moving parts of the cabinet—the door and the drawer—are now completed (**6–57** and **6–58**). At this point, you can nail the ¼-inch plywood back into the rabbeted opening in the cabinet back.

6–55. *Inserting the drawer slightly with the stop in the closed position.*

6–56. *Reaching in and putting the stop in the open position.*

6–57. *The drawer and door installed on the cabinet.*

6–58. *A smoothly working drawer is an indicator of fine cabinetwork.*

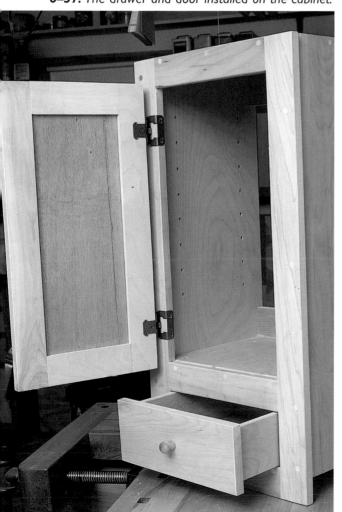

Installation Techniques

7–1. *Two cabinets stacked on top of each other: a hutch.*

▶Many cabinets you'll want to build will be freestanding. Media cabinets, hutches (**7–1**), chests of drawers, etc., are all meant to stand on legs. Perhaps the most important thing to remember when you build one of these is to assemble and stand it up to dry on a level surface. I use the table-saw top for this. With a very large freestanding cabinet, I lay a sheet of plywood over sawhorses. After assembly of freestanding cabinets, I stand the piece upright to dry and make sure all four legs are contacting the flat surface.

For mounting a cabinet on a wall, there are several options. A very lightweight cabinet, or shadow box (under three pounds), can be hung like a framed picture: with screw eyes, wire, and a nail or hanger in the wall. For wall cabinets of considerable size and weight, secure fastening to wall studs is essential.

Permanent wall-cabinet installation, like kitchen-cabinet installation, is usually obtained by screwing through the hanging rail in the back of the cabinet directly into the wall studs

(**7–2**). Another method is to screw 1 x 4-inch "cleats" to the wall studs. These cleats go at the correct height on the wall, and correspond to the position of the hanging rails on the cabinets (**7–3** and **7–4**). This second method eliminates the need of hitting a specific stud with the screw while holding the cabinet in position on the wall.

Hanging kitchen cabinets is a specialty all to itself, and certainly beyond the scope of this

7–2. Two massive wood screws are seen here securing this upper kitchen cabinet directly to wall studs.

7–4. The cabinet hung in position.

7–3 (left). Angled cleats screwed to the wall can receive cabinets (or anything else—like the clamp rack to the left) at two heights. At right is a cabinet ready for hanging.

book. It is more a carpenter's task than a cabinetmaker's, although many cabinetmakers install their own kitchen cabinets. It is absolutely essential that care and attention be paid to the installation of wall cabinets with regard to locating and screwing into the wall studs. Be sure you screw into the studs. A kitchen cabinet full of dishes can weigh hundreds of pounds and is extremely dangerous if it should fall off the wall. If you've never done this before, consult a trained professional before you attempt to hang kitchen cabinets. In my kitchen cabinet work, I often subcontract a carpenter to do the installation.

For single cabinets, it is possible to secure a wall cabinet to a wall by hanging it by a single screw anchored to a wall stud. A better solution is to use angled hanging cleats, as discussed below.

▼ ANGLED HANGING CLEATS

Angled hanging cleats are pieces of scrap plywood (**7–5**). They are slightly shorter than the width of the cabinet

and three or four inches wide. Both have one edge cut at 45 degrees, and the two pieces lock into each other. At the bottom of the cabinet is a spacer piece that is the same thickness as the upper hanging cleat, so the cabinet will rest plumb on the wall (**7–6**).

To hang a cabinet this way, first screw one of the hanging cleats to the cabinet back (**7–7**). Be sure the orientation of the cleat is correct, and that it's positioned just below where the rabbet starts. With 1¼-inch screws, screw the cleat through the ¼-inch plywood and into the top hanging rail. Screw the spacer piece to the lower rail also (**7–8**).

Once you've figured the location and height of

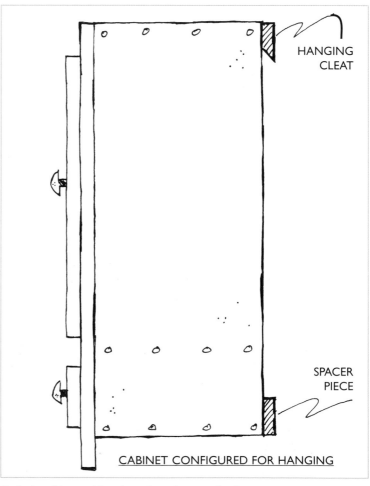

HANGING CLEAT

SPACER PIECE

CABINET CONFIGURED FOR HANGING

7–5. Two hanging cleats cut at 45 degrees.

7–6. A cabinet with a hanging cleat, and a lower spacer piece.

the cabinet, find a wall stud or studs and screw the other cleat into it. Be sure the cleat is level on the wall, and that the orientation is correct so the other cleat will lock into it. Again, be sure this cleat is secure—anchored to a wall stud. You can apply a simple molding to the cabinet sides to hide the cleats if you wish.

In my woodworking shop I have angled cleats, at two heights, running the length of every wall (**7–9**). This allows me to position all my cabinets anywhere I want to, with the ability to reposition them anywhere I want to, at any time.

7–7. Screwing the hanging cleat to the cabinet.

7–8. Screwing the spacer to the cabinet.

7–9. All the upper cabinets, racks, etc., in my workshop are hung on long, angled cleats (visible on the left and right). I can reposition them anywhere at any time.

CHAPTER

8

Finishing Techniques

Before applying any finish, it may be a good idea to sand the entire outside of the cabinet assembly with an orbital sander and fine-grit sandpaper—150 or 220. This will get it in good shape for applying a finish. Be sure to wipe the assembly clear of dust with a clean rag.

Finishing is a subject that can be unduly complicated and misleading. As is the case with most things, the simplest approach for finishing a cabinet is best. It is not recommended that wood stain be used. It's unnatural and looks phony (most home-center stains have almost no pigment in them, anyway). If a dark-wood effect is wanted, use dark wood for the cabinet and add a clear oil finish over it. Hardwood plywood is available in many different veneers, including darker woods.

▼ OIL FINISHES

Oil finishes are the easiest finish to use and look the nicest. The ones I prefer are the Danish- and tung-oil finishes (**8–1**). Application methods vary somewhat, but generally the surface is flooded with oil (**8–2**), left for about 20 minutes, and then the oil is wiped off (**8–3**). This procedure is repeated, and after about ten hours the cabinet is done. Instructions are provided with the product.

I like oil finishes primarily because they allow the wood to look simple and natural. Don't use oil finishes inside cabinets or drawers.

▼ WAX

Wax is a very nice, simple finish for furniture, used by itself or with other finishes. There are all types of waxes available for woodworking (**8–4**), and woodworking suppliers and catalogs offer an extensive selection. Wax allows for a natural-looking glossy finish for woods.

I use a paste wax that is made up of different types of waxes. It dries to a clear, hard, glossy finish. I use it only occasionally, but you may like it for a shinier look than can be provided with oil finish alone.

If you use wax over an oil finish, make sure the oil finish is completely dry—wait twice as

8–1. Oil finishes are easy to use and give the wood a natural look.

8–2. Flooding the wood surface with Danish oil.

8–3. After 30 minutes or so, the oil is wiped off with a clean rag.

8–4. Use a high-quality furniture wax. Some inexpensive waxes are made up of petroleum byproducts (sludge).

long as the label says. The wax is spread very thinly with a soft cloth. When it turns to a dull haze, wipe it off in a buffing motion with a clean, soft cloth. You can apply more than one coat if you want a very glossy look.

Wax can be applied inside cabinets also, and looks very nice when applied to raw wood (no previous finish). Use a tinted wax (which has some dark pigment in it) for darker woods like walnut (**8–5**); otherwise, white flecks will show in the wood grain.

▼ POLYURETHANE VARNISH

Polyurethane varnish is my least-favorite finish. It leaves an artificial-looking, "plastic" finish on the wood. It reminds me of wood-grained contact paper. Nonetheless, some people prefer polyurethane finishes, and I use it occasionally for commercial jobs like grocery-store installations and retail displays.

The easiest polyurethane to use is water-based. Water-based polyurethane dries fast and cleans up easily with soap and water. Some brands of water-based polyurethanes are very poor, but the Old Master brand seems satisfactory. Use a good-quality brush and apply the finish in three light coats (**8–6**).

Between coats, I like to lightly sand the finish with 220-grit sandpaper (**8–7**). I wipe it down with a clean rag, and then apply another coat. Before the last coat, use a tack rag to remove all the last traces of dust (**8–8**).

After opening a can of water-

based polyurethane, I transfer the contents into glass jars (**8–9**). This keeps the material fresh. The original cans can be difficult to open after the initial use, and rust can form around the rim of the lid, dropping rust particles into the material.

8–5. Some different tints of furniture wax.

8–6. When applying polyurethane, use a good-quality brush and apply the finish in three light coats.

8–7. Between coats, I like to lightly sand the finish with 220-grit sandpaper.

8–8. I wipe the polyurethane with a clean rag, and then apply another coat. Before the last coat, use a tack rag to remove all the last traces of dust.

8–9. High-quality water-based polyurethane. Many polyurethanes available in home centers are of very poor quality. After opening the can, I transfer the contents to glass jars.

8–10. The cabinet oiled and waxed.

Epilogue

In the preceding pages, you've built one specific cabinet in order to become familiar with my cabinetmaking method. The cabinet is a relatively small wall unit with one shelf and one drawer. The size and design of the unit are based on practical considerations: it's not too big to be unmanageable; nor is it too small to show the technique properly.

Once you understand the cabinetmaking process, you can build any size cabinets, for any function you like. What follows are some general guidelines for a few types of cabinets.

▼ FURNITURE

The method of cabinetmaking described in this book (biscuits and screws) can be used for any type of furniture you choose to make, including chests of drawers, hutches, side tables, wall cupboards (**E–1**), etc. It can be used for any furniture design requiring a carcass assembly.

A chest of drawers, for example, is a cabinet with legs, drawers, and a top. The drawers and face frame are made the same way as described in the book, and side guides and kickers align the drawer. But furniture drawers usually ride on frames rather than extend over an entire piece, as the drawer for my cabinet does. The frames save money and weight, especially on larger furniture. Frame members, being usually 2½ inches wide **x** ¾ inch thick, are less costly than a full sheet of materials, and less material also equals less weight.

Biscuit joints can be used to join frames to the carcass as long as plywood is used as the carcass material. Solid-wood panels will eventually crack. They will move against the rigid frames. The very best cabinetmakers solve this problem by joining the frames to the carcass sides with sliding dovetail joints. Best (easiest) cut by hand, the sliding dovetail joint holds the frames very securely while still allowing for wood movement.

Furniture with doors and face frames can be handled the same way as described in the book.

E–1. *These two wall cabinets hang above a row of base cabinets in the workshop—and are just one of the many types that can be built using the cabinetmaking techniques described in the previous chapters.*

▼ BOOKCASES

A bookcase (**E–2**) is simply a tall, open carcass. Best made of plywood, it is a good choice for the biscuit-and-screw method of cabinetmaking. A bookcase has no face frame or door. A permanent shelf should be installed at the middle of the bookcase height to prevent the sides from bowing out. Holes can be drilled for adjustable shelves for pins used to hold them as described in the book. Bookcases should never be wider than about 20 inches, or the shelves will sag.

Because the components are plywood, veneer tape can be used to cover the plies on the edges. It is also perfectly acceptable to round over and sand exposed plies on the edges of the plywood.

▼ KITCHEN CABINETS

Kitchen cabinets are a bit more utilitarian, and a little less fancy than fine furniture. For this reason, among others, drawers are usually operated with prefabricated metal slides. These are available in a great many styles and specifications. They work and wear quite well, but are inappropriate for fine furniture.

Kitchen base cabinets (**E–3** and **E–4**) rest on the floor, as opposed to wall cabinets or "uppers," which hang on the wall. Kitchen base cabinets have a "toe kick" at the bottom front to allow for your feet to move slightly under the unit as you stand at it. Base cabinets almost always have a shallow drawer over a door below, or can be an entire bank of four drawers, from shallow on up to deeper drawers below.

Kitchen base cabinets are almost always 24 inches deep and 36 inches high. There is no standard or "normal" width for kitchen cabinets. However, one wider than about 27 inches is awkward. It opens out too far into the room.

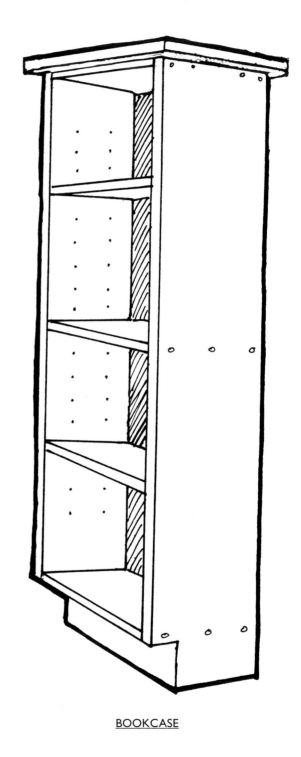

BOOKCASE

E–2. A bookcase, a tall, open carcass with no face frame or door, can be built using the cabinetmaking techniques described in previous chapters.

Upper kitchen cabinets are much like the cabinet made for this book, although they usually don't have drawers. They are all usually about 12 inches deep. I don't like doors for upper cabinets to be wider than about 12 to 15 inches. They can smack you in the head as they're opened. For a wider cabinet, say 30 inches, I make two doors that overlap or fit to a center face-frame stile.

Upper kitchen cabinets can be drilled for adjustable shelves. Depending on your needs, you may want two or more per cabinet. "Standard" American dinner dishes will fit in a 12-inch-deep cabinet (with a 12-inch opening, of course). Be sure to size any dishes, platters, etc., for upper cabinets before you build them. Much of the beautiful dinnerware made in Mexico, for example, is oversized and won't fit into a standard cabinet.

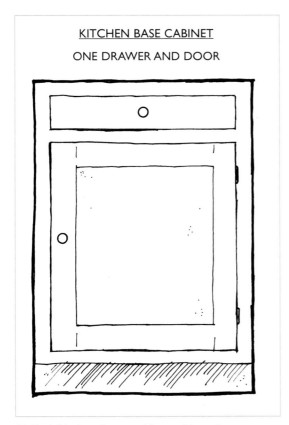

E–3. *A kitchen base cabinet with a drawer above a door.*

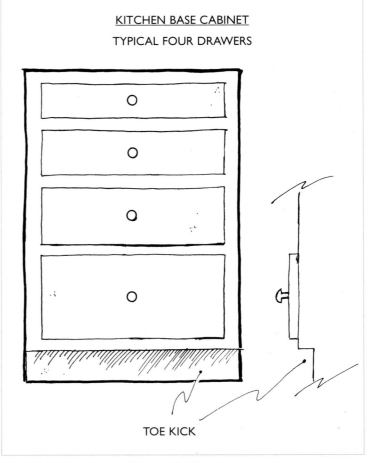

E–4. *A kitchen base cabinet with four drawers.*

E-5. A wide, two-door upper utility cabinet in my workshop. Note the plugs.

▼ UTILITY CABINETS

For laundry rooms, workshops, garages, sewing rooms, etc., a utility cabinet is used (**E–5**). These are essentially kitchen-type units made from lesser-quality materials. Many times, old, battered kitchen cabinets are used as utility cabinets. For shop cabinets, I use whatever plywood scrap is lying around from other jobs, and usually I skip the finishing steps. For use inside a home, utility cabinets should be made of appropriate high-quality material and finished to look nice.

▼ BATHROOM CABINETS

Bathrooms, of course, are usually small, so you have to size cabinets accordingly to ensure that people can fit in there, too (**E–6**). Medicine chests, for example, are four inches deep or less. All other height and width specifications must be determined by the requirements of the specific job

E-6. This bathroom cabinet was built to hold linens, towels, etc.

METRIC EQUIVALENTS CHART

INCHES TO MILLIMETERS AND CENTIMETERS
MM— Millimeters   CM—Centimeters

INCHES	MM	CM	INCHES	CM	INCHES	CM
⅛	3	0.3	9	22.9	30	76.2
¼	6	0.6	10	25.4	31	78.7
⅜	10	1.0	11	27.9	32	81.3
½	13	1.3	12	30.5	33	83.8
⅝	16	1.6	13	33.0	34	86.4
¾	19	1.9	14	35.6	35	88.9
⅞	22	2.2	15	38.1	36	91.4
1	25	2.5	16	40.6	37	94.0
1¼	32	3.2	17	43.2	38	96.5
1½	38	3.8	18	45.7	39	99.1
1¾	44	4.4	19	48.3	48	101.6
2	51	5.1	20	50.8	41	104.1
2½	64	6.4	21	53.3	42	106.7
3	76	7.6	22	55.9	43	109.2
3½	89	8.9	23	58.4	44	111.8
4	102	10.2	24	61.0	45	114.3
4½	114	11.4	25	63.5	46	116.8
5	127	12.7	25	66.0	47	119.4
6	152	15.2	27	68.6	48	121.9
7	178	17.8	28	71.1	49	124.5
8	203	20.3	29	73.7	50	127.0

Glossary

Backstop Small hardwood piece that limits drawer travel into the cabinet.

Base Cabinet A cabinet that rests on the floor.

Belt Sander A sander with an abrasive belt that is held in tension between two rollers. It can quickly remove material.

Bench-Top Saw A light table saw that could be lifted and carried to the job site. It should always be used clamped or bolted down.

Biscuit Joint A spline joint made with a biscuit jointer (a dedicated machine) and prefabricated, compressed hardwood plates (biscuits). The biscuit joint is fast to make and has great strength.

Biscuit Jointer (also referred to as a biscuit joiner or plate joiner) A portable power tool with a grinder-like motor housing and a sliding carriage. Its job is to accurately plunge biscuit slots into the work.

Biscuits (also referred to as splines or plates) Thin, football-shaped wooden pieces that are used to join the slots or grooves cut by the jointer. They come in a variety of sizes.

Butt Chisel A chisel that has a slightly thicker and shorter blade than a bench chisel. The shorter blade permits the hands to hold the chisel in close to the work. In plywood cabinetwork, it is useful for trimming biscuits or plugs, squaring up rabbets in cabinet backs, and trimming grooves.

Cabinet Saw A heavy, professional table saw, usually with a blade at least 10 inches in diameter, a large motor, and heavy castings enclosed in a standing cabinet.

Carcass The basic box of a cabinet.

Checks Small cracks on the surface of solid boards.

Chest of Drawers Furniture designed for drawer storage. It is essentially a cabinet with drawers, a top, and sometimes legs.

Clamping Stands T-shaped accessories used in pairs when clamping face frames or doors. The assembly is laid across the clamping stands. With the clamps hung underneath, diagonals are easy to check (for square). This also helps ensure the assembly dries flat.

Cleats For hanging cabinets, interlocking 45-degree angled pieces--one on the cabinet, one on the wall.

Combination Square A very versatile measuring tools with a 45- and 90-degree sliding head.

Contractor's Saw A general-purpose table saw mounted on an integral stand, good for all but the most heavy work.

Countersink To set the head of a screw at or below the surface of the workpiece.

Crosscut A cut across the grain of the wood.

Dado Head A blade and chipper assembly used on a table saw to cut grooves, rabbets, notches, etc.

Dado Joint A joint often used in making shelves or cross members. It should always be shouldered.

Danish Oil A penetrating oil finish.

Dividers A measuring tool used to lay out circles and to transfer measurements. They often have two sharp, pointed metal legs.

Dovetail Joint A strong two-part joint that consists of a tail and a mating pin. It is often used in drawers.

Dovetail Saw A small handsaw with a turned handle. It is also referred to as a Gent's Saw, and is also available with a foxtail handle.

Drawer Stop A piece used to prevent the drawer from being pulled completely out of the opening.

Edge-Jointing Making the edges of boards straight and square, usually to glue them together.

End Grain Exposed open cells on the ends of a board. Not a glue surface.

Face Frame A frame fastened to the front of the carcass and to which a door is usually hinged.

Face-Jointing The process of flattening the face of a board. This can be done with a jointer or a hand plane.

Fence Either integral or removable, an alignment accessory at the front of the biscuit jointer's sliding carriage.

Fixed-Base Router A router designed to keep the bit at one fixed vertical position throughout the operation.

Folding Rule A rigid measuring ruler that folds for storage.

Frame Joint A joint used on picture frames, face and door frames, etc. In the method discussed in this book, a biscuit joint is used instead of the more traditional mortise-and-tenon joint.

Frame-and-Panel Door Construction in which the panels float in slots or rabbets in the frame members.

Gent's Saw See Dovetail Saw.

Glass-and-Mirror Door A frame-and-panel door in which glass is used instead of the 1/4-inch panel. This type of door is useful for display and medicine cabinets.

Glue Bottle A bottle made for gluing biscuit joints. It has a nozzle that spreads the glue on the correct surfaces (sides) of the biscuit slots. Fast, accurate, indispensable (for me).

Grain Direction The orientation of the fibers in wood.

Grooves Channels cut into a wood surface.

Hanging Rails Rails that go in the upper and lower back of the cabinet and allow it to be anchored to a wall.

Hardboard A sheet material made from compressed wood fibers. Also called Masonite.

Hardwood Woods from broad-leaved trees, such as cherry, mahogany, oak, walnut, etc. Tulip (poplar) and soft maple are good choices for the projects in this book.

Hutch A utility cupboard, traditionally used in kitchens or dining rooms. A functional chest on chest.

Jack Plane A general-purpose hand plane that is approximately 12 to 17 inches long. In cabinetmaking, it is used to shave off and straighten table-saw marks left on solid wood and to flatten any surface irregularities where the stiles and rails join.

Jointer A stationary power tool used to square and true solid-wood boards. I mention in the book that a jointer can be used to remove marks made by the table saw, but the jointer marks will then have to be removed by sanding or planing.

Jointer Plane A 23- to 24-inch plane that will obtain a flat surface on the longest boards, whether on an edge or the face. A jointer plane or a jack plane can be used to shave off and straighten table-saw marks left on solid wood and to flatten any surface irregularities where the stiles and rails join.

Jointing Making an edge straight and square with the face of the board.

Kerf The cut made by a saw blade.

Kickers Pieces installed above the cabinet drawer to prevent it from dropping down as it's opened.

Kitchen Base Cabinets Kitchen cabinets that rest on the floor. They are almost always 24 inches deep and 36 inches high.

Knockdown Furniture Furniture that is designed to be assembled and disassembled many times.

Knot The base of a branch, apparent in sawn solid wood. Solid wood is used for the face and door frames of the cabinets described in this book.

Leaf Hinge Hinge with two thin plates drilled and countersunk for screws, moving radially along a pin and knuckle axis.

Linseed-Oil Finish A simple, penetrating oil finish.

Marking Gauge A tool used to lay out lines parallel to the edges on a board. The best type are of the Japanese design, which uses a blade for marking.

Marking Knife A sharp knife used to mark out joinery or dimensioning cuts.

Masonite Fiberboard made from steam-exploded wood fiber. It is recommended for shim pieces when using a biscuit jointer to cut cabinet drawer pieces. Also known as hardboard.

Media Cabinets Entertainment centers holding VCRs and television sets and/or CD/vinyl record/tape storage and audio equipment.

Medicine Chests Cabinets four inches deep or less that are used in bathrooms, usually with a mirrored door.

Miter Joint A joint made by fastening pieces together at a 45-degree angle.

Molding A wood-surface shape or a narrow strip that is used primarily for decoration. Moldings are also used to hide things, usually mistakes!

Mortise Gauge Similar to a marking gauge, a tool with a fence and two beams that is used to mark mortises and tenons. It can also be used for other markings.

Mortise Jig See Router Jig.

Mortise-and-Tenon Joint A very strong joint in which the mortise (hole) is cut into one piece and the tenon (mating piece) fits into the slot. The joints used on cabinet faces and door frames are traditionally mortise-and-tenon joints. The cabinets discussed in this book are built with biscuit joints, which have advantages over mortise-and-tenon joints.

Nail Set A tool used to push a brad deeper than a hammer can reach.

Oil Finish A waterproof finish that penetrates the wood and allows a natural (nongloss) look to the wood. It is recommended for use on cabinets.

Orbital Sander The most versatile finish sander. A

sander with a square pad that takes standard sheet sandpaper and moves in a tiny, rapid circular pattern to smooth surfaces. Unlike a random orbit sander, the orbital sander is very good for rounding over sharp edges on face frames and doors. It can also sand into corners.

Overlap Hinges Hinges that allow the door to overlap the cabinet to which they are attached. They are the hinges of choice for the cabinets described in this book. Very forgiving!

Panel-Cutting Jig A shop-made jig used to cut wide panels of plywood or solid wood. My design has the advantage of keeping the blade visible at all times. Unlike other crosscut jigs, the blade will not dangerously emerge from a hidden position under the jig.

Particleboard A sheet material made from pressed wood chips or wood particles. This material makes good use of what otherwise would be waste material.

Pegboard Material with regularly spaced perforations into which hooks may be inserted to store or display items. The jig used to make the adjustable shelf holes described in this book is made of pegboard.

Plane Hand tool used to smooth wood surfaces. In plywood cabinetmaking, it is used to shave off table-saw marks left on solid wood and to correct surface irregularities.

Planer A power tool used to surface lumber and dimension it to proper thickness.

Plunge Router A router that features vertical bit movement with the power on.

Plywood A sheet material made by gluing together thin layers of wood. Hardwood – veneer plywood is the recommended material for cabinet carcasses. Birch is good looking and not too expensive.

Polyurethane Varnish A finish that leaves an artificial-looking, "plastic" film on wood. It is not my recommended finish for cabinets, except in some professional applications.

PVA (Polyvinyl Acetate) Glue Modern yellow or white glues. They are nontoxic, inexpensive, clean up easily with water, and have strong bonding qualities.

Pyramid Marks A system of marks made on face-frame, carcass, and door pieces so the cabinetmaker can keep track of the top, bottom, left and right sides, and shelf pieces.

Quick-Change Countersink Accessory A drilling accessory used to drill and counterbore holes in the face frame and carcass of a cabinet. The best ones have easily replaceable drills.

Rabbet Bit An edge-forming bit with a piloted end that makes an L-shaped cut along an edge or end of a board.

Rabbet Joint An L-shaped channel that goes along the edge of a piece of stock.

Rails The horizontal members of a frame or panel. This is easy to remember: a railroad track is always horizontal.

Retaining Clips Clips used on the glass of glass-and-mirror doors that allow the glass or mirror to be replaced in case of damage.

Reveal An intentional trim gap. The most common use of reveal is between an entry doorjamb and casework.

Rip Cut A cut made with the grain of the wood.

Roundover Bit One of the many kinds of edge-forming bit with a piloted end that converts square edges, ends, and corners of a board to a convex radius. A roundover bit gives a plain, elegant edge treatment.

Router Portable power tool with a cutting instrument that cuts the surface or edge of wood. It can be either a plunge type or fixed-base.

Router Jig (Mortise Jig) A shop-made jig that can be used to accurately rout grooves in rails and stiles for frame-and-panel doors.

Router Table Any routing system in which the router is mounted upside down beneath a flat surface so that the bit protrudes vertically through this surface. The best ones have easy-to-operate controls, are not too big and heavy, and have enough power for most routing jobs.

Shadow Box A deep picture frame. It is also a tiny, open-faced cabinet.

Sheet Stock Man-made wood material sold in sheets 4 feet wide and 8 to 12 feet long. Common types of sheet stock include plywood, particleboard, hardboard, and paneling.

Shoulder The "buttress" of any good woodworking joint. It creates mechanical strength by minimizing or eliminating "racking," in which a joint comes out of square on all four corners. Biscuit joints are almost all shoulder and are a strong joint to use on cabinets, both for glue surface and mechanical strength.

Sliding Dovetail A dovetail-shaped dado joint, very useful in solid-wood carcass construction (solid wood moves), that is glued on one end. An unusual mixture of great strength and allowance for wood movement.

Slots Variously shaped channels such as mortises, dadoes, and grooves that are cut into wood.

Softwood Wood from trees that bear needles rather than broad leaves. Pine and fir are commonly used softwoods.

Square Parts that are at right (90-degree) angles to each other; also, a box or frame in the condition of having all four corners at 90 degrees.

Squaring Blocks Shop-made accessories that are spring-clamped to the insides of cabinets to keep them square during assembly and while they dry.

Stack Dado Head Blade-and-chipper set that is used on a table saw to cut grooves, rabbets, etc. It is the most accurate head, but the most time-consuming to set up.

Stiles A vertical member of a frame or panel.

Stop Block A shop-made accessory used in conjunction with a panel cutter on a table saw. It allows the cabinetmaker to make repeatable cuts for cabinet face frames and door parts.

Storypole A shop-made stick with dimensions marked on it. This allows dimensions to be made directly from a piece of furniture, a room, or plans to the stick; then the dimensions are transferred to the workpieces via the stick. It is more accurate than measuring.

Straightedge A piece of material with a straight edge for testing straight lines and surfaces or drawing straight lines.

Stud Usually a 2 x 4-foot upright in wall framing to which the wall sheathing is attached.

Table Saw A stationary power tool with a circular-saw blade that can be used to make rip and crosscuts, to resaw, cut rabbets and rabbets, and perform many other operations.

Tear-Out Displaced wood fibers caused from a blade or bit exiting the cut without backing.

Tempered Glass Glass treated so as to have increased strength and to shatter into small pieces when broken. Tempered glass is recommended for use on glass-and-mirror cabinet doors.

Toe Kick A part of a kitchen base cabinet located on the bottom front that allows feet to move slightly under the unit while the person is standing at it. Frank Klaus simply calls this the "kick."

Tung Oil A natural oil derived from the seeds of the Chinese tung tree. It is used by itself or mixed with other oils to make penetrating oil finishes.

Utility Cabinets Essentially kitchen cabinets used from lesser-quality materials, these cabinets are used in laundry rooms, workshops, garages, etc.

Utility Knife A knife with a replaceable, often retractable, blade. It is most often used for heavy work.

Veneer-Core Plywood Plywood with usually three to nine veneer plies. It is stronger than solid-lumber core or medium-density-fiberboard-core plywood and is the recommended material for cabinet carcasses.

Vise The part of the bench used to hold boards. Depending on the vise used, the boards can be held on edge, end up, or flat on the bench top.

Wax A simple-to-use finish that provides a natural-looking glossy look on woods. It can be applied to raw wood and to the inside of cabinets.

White Glue PVA glue. It has a longer drying time and is more "rubbery" than yellow glue. Either is fine.

Wobble Dado Head Single-blade head used on a table saw to cut grooves in face frames and carcasses. It is somewhat less accurate than the stack dado head, but is much faster to set up and adjust.

Wood Veneer Tape A very thin strip of wood backed with strong paper that comes in a variety of wood types. The glue is heat-activated. This material is best used on plywood to cover and dress up the exposed plies.

Workpiece The piece of wood or stock that is being cut.

Yellow Glue PVA (polyvinyl acetate) glue. It sets faster and is more brittle than white PVA glue (so as to sand easier).

Zeroing Out Setting the router bit's position and locking the bit in position where its end just touches the work surface. From here, depth adjustments are made.

Index

About the Author

Anthony Guidice is a furnituremaker, teacher, and writer living in Rochester, New York. Contributing editor to *Woodwork Magazine* and author of *The Seven Essentials of Woodworking*, Anthony also conducts workshops and seminars on woodworking.